SULTAN

ELIZABETH AVEDON EDITIONS

VINTAGE CONTEMPORARY ARTISTS

D0402192

VINTAGE BOOKS

A DIVISION OF RANDOM HOUSE NEW YORK

A Vintage Contemporary Artists Original, November 1988
FIRST EDITION

Library of Congress Cataloging-in-Publication Data

Sultan, Donald.
Sultan.

(Vintage contemporary artists)
"An interview with Donald Sultan by Barbara Rose"—P.
"Elizabeth Avedon editions."
1. Sultan, Donald—Interviews.   2. Artists—United States—Interviews.
I. Rose, Barbara.   II. Title.   III. Series.
N6537.S92A2   1988   709'.2'4   88-40176
ISBN 0-394-74793-3 (pbk.)

COVER PHOTOGRAPH © 1988 BY RICHARD AVEDON

BACK COVER: *Pears on a Branch Feb. 3, 1988.*
Tar, spackle and oil on tile over Masonite; 96" x 96".
Courtesy Blum Helman Gallery, Inc., New York.
Photo: Bill Jacobson Studio.

Manufactured in the United States of America
10   9   8   7   6   5   4   3   2   1

AN INTERVIEW
WITH
DONALD SULTAN
BY BARBARA ROSE

INTRODUCTION

At thirty-seven, Donald Sultan is one of the most respected as well as one of the more controversial contemporary American painters. Born in Asheville, North Carolina, Sultan was the second of four children of a Rumanian Jewish family. His paternal grandfather had emigrated from Russia to New York, then to Detroit to work in the auto factories, seeking a better life in the promised land of America. Today, Sultan's cultured Southern accent, polished good manners, intellectual interests and Francophilia imply generations of ease, which may explain why no one relates the decaying and ruined industrial landscapes he paints with the actuality of assembly-line Detroit his grandfather experienced. But it is typical of Donald Sultan's coolly controlled persona—which may mask a myriad of real doubts behind a façade of apparently unassailable self-assurance—that he would never claim proletarian origins any more than would Renoir. Nevertheless, it is of interest that like Andy Warhol, the son of a Czech steelworker, and Neil Jenny, whose parents worked in the now defunct Massachusetts textile mills, Sultan has a direct tie to a now vanishing industrial America. By the time Sultan's father, an aspiring painter who despaired of making a living by his work, had established a thriving tire business in the small North Carolina mountain town, there was enough money to give Donald, who showed talent for both art and theater, the finest education.

At fifteen, he was sent away to prep school in New England, although he later returned to study art, philosophy and theater at the prestigious and intellectually demanding University of North Carolina at Chapel Hill. By the time he graduated, he had decided to pursue the vocation that his father, who had taken him to museums for years and taught him to love and respect art, never felt confident enough to pursue. He was accepted into the difficult, competitive MFA program at the Art Institute of Chicago, where Claes Oldenburg was also trained. The dominant Chicago style has always been characteristically figurative and expressionistic; true to his contradictory nature, Sultan at first rejected both. Ultimately, however, he would become a painter of recognizable images for basically the same reason that Oldenburg chose to make objects: because most people see images even in abstract shapes.

Like Oldenburg, Johns and Jenney, Sultan uses simple, familiar images reduced to their most generic schematization, so that they act more as condensed signs than as fully developed illusionistic representations. In the context of the development of a new imagistic art that reduced representation to painted, textured signs rather than imitating the reproduced, flat, graphic look of pop art, one should also mention Philip Guston, the Abstract Expressionist who renounced abstraction as too remote a form of communication in the last brilliant decade of his life, which was when Donald Sultan arrived in New York.

An avant-garde painter not yet fully committed to the exigent, disciplined aesthetic of modernism, which he would ultimately redefine in terms of his own personal vision, Sultan had already helped organize an alternative art space in Chicago, the N.A.M.E. Gallery, where his own early efforts at manipulating materials and objects in assemblage works were shown. He also published artists' writings and helped organize group activities, which is typical of his activist, confrontational temperament. In 1977, he had his first solo show in New York at P.S. 1. The title of one review was "Like the Floor of Old Kitchens." By that time, Sultan was already painting on one-foot-square standard linoleum tile, a cheap, easily available industrial modular material like Carl Andre's square metal floor plates, whose grids they recall, and Dan Flavin's standard fluorescent tubing. The big difference was the degree of artistic transformation Sultan performed on his materials, and the fact that they were neither ephemeral nor mutable. The obvious fakeness of linoleum imitating granite or marble, with its seamy Tobacco Road connotations, was contradicted by the artist's intervention, which required gluing these squares permanently into a Mondrian-like grid on Masonite and covering them with pigment, a brackish-colored, unpleasantly sticky mixture of industrial materials he was familiar with from childhood, such as tar and rubber, liquified to pouring and spreading consistency.

Gradually, Sultan has added to his initial vocabulary of images of common objects, as well as to his technical mastery of his unconventional media. Looking and reading have made him a self-conscious modernist, almost a tautology since an essential feature of modernism is its painfully developed degree of self-consciousness. This has led Sultan to emphasize the distinct qualities of the various elements of painting: the surface (the plastic tile squares glued together into a grid); the support (the Masonite ground into which the tiles are inlaid), which is then projected forward so that the viewer is conscious of its artificiality; and the presence of the redundant stretcher bars behind the supporting ground, which in fact serve no practical purpose except to identify the material object as a painting belonging to a tradition of stretched paintings and gridded formats that Cubism inherited from classical art.

That the single "holistic" image is obviously made of parts or fragments forced to cohere through the will of the artist to present an image of wholeness and integrity may be interpreted as a moral as well as an aesthetic statement. The vaguely discernible grid formed by the edges of the modular tiles is also a tautological reference to the means by which academic painters transferred their "cartoons," i.e., preliminary drawings, to canvas to be filled in with paint. With a consistent sense of rebuttal, Sultan then ignores the grid: his floral bouquets, fruit still lifes and landscapes fill with an impressive monumentality the entire field of the painting, as opposed to the rhyming analogous shapes of classical and Cubist art. Overlapping rectangular boundaries, Sultan seems to be putting forth a philosophical argument against the need to polarize linear and painterly, classical and baroque compositions as articulated by the great Swiss art historian, Heinrich Wölfflin.

Is Sultan kidding, having his cake and eating it too? Or is this a serious attempt to redefine painting as a synthesis of traditions with great potential within the strict and not easily expanded discipline of modernism? It seems to me the latter is the case, especially since we see the artist constantly straining against his own best efforts, pushing himself to take on more and more difficult tasks, e.g., larger paintings that require canvas supports and an even more complex attitude toward media and technique, including the use of oil paint. For although Donald Sultan has a decisive personal style, a select and limited vocabulary of images he has claimed as his own, there is really no telling where he will take the art to which he is fully committed. To confront the best efforts of the masters of past time, to claim there is much left for painting, indeed for modernist painting, at a moment in which many artists flourish by abdicating any sense of responsibility toward the past or the future, seems to me an act of exemplary courage.

Sultan's experiments with media and techniques are not attempts to be novel or shocking, but are a means to create formal innovation. The idea that technical innovation was the breakthrough to formal innovation was introduced by John Graham, mentor of the Abstract Expressionists, in his book *System and Dialectic of Art*. The theory deeply influenced Jackson Pollock, whose paintings with shapes cut out of the painting surface to reveal the support are what Sultan is grappling with in his inlaid and cut-out portions of canvas filled in with plaster or vinyl. In focusing on these critical "cut-out" paintings of Pollock's, Sultan has solved the problem that ultimately defeated Pollock: he has reconciled advanced modernist painting with figuration without sacrificing painterliness or surface texture. This is a large and significant achievement.

In his life-style (he is still married to his college sweetheart; they have two children), his separations of line and shadow and his love of genres, Sultan resembles Monet or Matisse rather than the undisciplined, deliberately unconventional artist the popular mind associates with the "vie de bohème." He seems more nineteenth-century Parisian than late-twentieth-century New York. His friends are artists, but also writers, actors and directors (his wife, Susan, is producing her first full-length feature film). He is acutely aware of the media saturation of the American mind, and determined both to acknowledge and to fight actively against its leveling and deadening effects. Sultan's paintings have a loaded iconography: the still lifes, for example, deal with erotic bulbous forms as well as with the potential for death implied in an artificially engineered environment. Almost all the landscapes he calls "events" are about disasters. They warn of the toxic poison floating in the haze of our ignorance of what creates chaos and breakdown in postindustrial civilization. A fuller reading of Sultan's iconography—and one wonders why it hasn't been undertaken, since that iconography is so richly provocative and relevant—would focus on the slippage between subject matter, content and form that takes place in a work of fine art created within the context of mass culture. To deal with these problems without becoming a symptom of them is not the least of the accomplishments of an artist who could well quote André Gide's advice to his critics: "Do not understand me too quickly."

COLOR PLATES

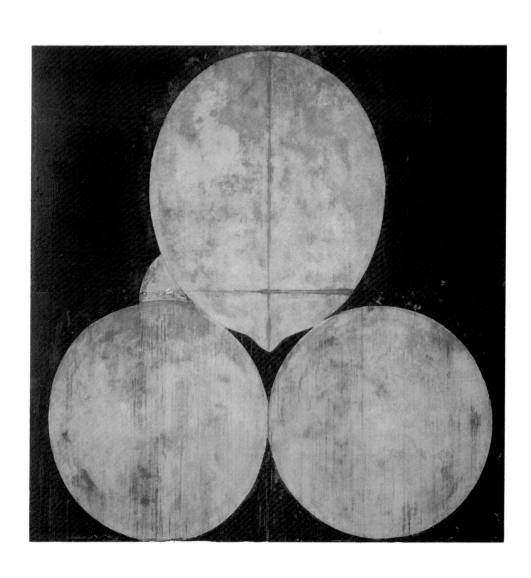

EARLY MORNING MAY 20, 1986.
Latex and tar on tile over Masonite; $9\frac{1}{2}''$ x 97".
Courtesy Blum Helman Gallery, Inc., New York.
Photo: Bill Jacoson Studio.

HYDRANGEA JAN. 15, 1988.
Tar, oil and spackle on tile over Masonite; 96" x 96"
Courtesy Blum Helman Gallery, Inc., New York.
Photo: Earl Ripling.

THREE LIMES AND AN ORANGE MAY 10, 1988.
Tar, spackle and oil on tile ove Masonite; 96" x 96".
Courtesy Blum Helman Gallery, Inc., New York.
Photo: Bill Jacobson Studio.

RIG NOV. 30, 2987.
Tar and latex on tile over Masonite; $96\frac{1}{2}''$ x $96\frac{1}{2}''$.
Courtesy Blum Helman Gallery, Inc., New York.
Photo: Earl Ripling.

THE INTERVIEW

BR: *Where were you born?*

DS: In the mountains of North Carolina—Asheville, North Carolina. I remember being surrounded by mountains; I don't have too many early memories. I never seemed to be that involved in my childhood. It's a funny thing—as a kid I always thought of myself as an adult. I never really felt like I quite fit in. I guess every kid feels that way. I don't remember my childhood as being a good or a bad experience. It seemed to be a time when you were just there. I do remember things about my father painting. He was pretty good. He used to tell me that's what he wanted to be. But after the war he felt that he couldn't earn a living being a painter, so he went into the business that my grandfather had started, which was a tire business. He had a tire shop across from the courthouse. On the wall of his office he had a collection of guns that had been made across the street in the jail or upstate in the prisons—concoctions that prisoners had made in the machine shop, handmade guns for escape.

BR: *How did that impress you?*

DS: I thought that those were the coolest-looking things. He had a gun that was made out of soap that a guy hand-carved to try to escape and pistols that really worked, that fired. The tire shop was sort of a dark place in the back. There was an Australian guy who used to buff the treads off the tires for retreading; all of these guys were ex-soldiers, very wiry, tough, toothless guys. He had an elevator in there where he stored tires; it was very similar to the elevator I have in my studio now. I remember the smell of that rubber, these really incredible smells. It's not so different from the rubber I use now. But you always think of these things later. He painted and he always had his place filled with pictures.

BR: *What kinds of paintings?*

DS: When I was real young he brought home the Jackson Pollock cover of *Life* and he went downstairs and started painting drip paintings. It was just around the house and he was painting it, because I was born in '51. I remember it being around and I remember him dripping. He tried everything—he painted Cubist paintings and tried frottage—all kinds of stuff. He had a little studio downstairs, he had easels and he tried to paint portraits of us. I have a couple of little paintings of his in my studio.

BR: *Maybe because your father was a painter you think being an artist is a normal activity, not anything special or different, just a kind of work.*

DS: Yes, but I do think of it as special. I've always thought of it as something special because he never tried to make a living at it. Although I think that he really would have. My mother tried to get us involved in the theater. Originally, I thought I was going to be an actor. We had a children's theater in Asheville that was pretty elaborate for a children's theater. I moved from that into summer theater.

BR: *That explains why it's easy for you to speak in public; most artists have difficulty expressing themselves or are terrified of being on stage.*

DS: I did a lot of acting. I thought that was what I was going to be; I went to Chapel Hill originally from school in Massachusetts, thinking that I would be in the theater department there. I was brought up in all boys' schools from the time I was in the fourth grade, first in the private Catholic schools in North Carolina. But they only went to the eighth grade. I went to public school for ninth grade. My brother had gone to public high school, so I went to the public junior high school for one year and I didn't like it at all. We found a boarding school in Massachusetts that would accept me. I was fifteen when I left home and I really never came back.

I had a South African roommate. I thought it was a great thing to be coming up to the North from the South because I grew up in a Southern environment. This was the sixties. In my town, too, there were enormous parts of the town, Biltmore Forest and the country clubs and all these places did not allow Jews. I always thought this was the weirdest thing and I thought, "Boy, now I'll go up North where they have no prejudice against races." And I never encountered such racism in my life. I was shocked by it.

BR: Do you think that being from the South has made any kind of difference in terms of your personality, your work, your themes?

DS: One thinks about the South a lot, its place in history and how it affects people and the differences between Southerners, but for Southerners it's almost impossible to tell.

BR: Was your family always from the South?

DS: My grandfather came over from Russia in 1917 and he moved to New York and lived on the Lower East Side. He did odd jobs, but he couldn't make a living and he didn't like it. He went to Detroit and worked on the assembly lines as so many people did. He met my grandmother, who was from the same village in Russia. They got married and she was diagnosed as having tuberculosis. Asheville, North Carolina, was a place where people went because of the altitude, so they moved to the mountains. My father was born in Detroit; they must have moved when he was young. During the Depression they made a living by going from Asheville to Detroit picking up old batteries off the side of the road and emptying the acid into buckets and selling the battery acid back to the car people in Detroit and vice versa. Then Grandfather started a scrap business and that's how they made a living in Asheville.

My mother's family was from New York City; I don't know why they moved down South. I think my grandfather opened a business down there. My mother was born in Norfolk, Virginia, and then moved to Asheville.

BR: When did you first start looking at paintings and become interested in art?

DS: I was always looking at paintings. My first sexual experience was with erotic drawings that I made. I remember taking art classes; I was always taking classes and drawing. Some of my projects in grammar school were drawing, painting. I would enter all of the art contests and never win. I had a show of prints at the Asheville Art Museum recently and a man introduced himself as my painting teacher when I was in seventh grade. When I was in theater, we painted sets and learned set design; you learned the techniques of using big brushes, working on things on scaffoldings. Painting was always a part of life for me; it wasn't a strange thing to have a brush.

BR: When did you decide not to be an actor and to be an artist?

DS: When I went to Chapel Hill I was enrolled in the drama school. I looked at the students there and I realized that I wasn't going to be able to deal with this.

BR: Why?

DS: I thought that the whole thing was too weird. For me, painting, like acting, was a natural thing and I did it naturally and I was good at it. Most of the people there were pretending, were very dramatic people, wearing capes and this and that. I thought, I can't learn anything in this place and I can't deal with these people. The very first day they said, "Look to your right, look to your left, one of you won't be here in four years," and I said to the guy sitting next to me, "Me," and I got up and left. Then I enrolled in the film and television department and I was very interested in that for a while. I formed a group with some older students, a kind of cooperative to work on each other's films and to help finance each other's films. I was very involved in television; we went to the stations and did live TV. We would write and make videos, but, again, I couldn't deal with the teachers.

BR: Do you think that that experience affected your work in any way?

DS: The problem was the money involved. I began to see that to make your own movies, you had to deal and go after people to raise money, so I gravitated to the painting department where I felt that I could have complete control over my own expression. I looked at paintings all the time during this period. I felt I wasn't seeing any paintings that I wanted to see, so I started working seriously as a painter. In my first drawing class I didn't think that I was doing very well. But my teacher told me that I could really draw, that I was a very good draftsman and that encouraged me. I started painting minimal paintings at that time—I didn't know anything about it—I would take a canvas and start applying one color over and over again until it was completely beige. I thought that was a great way of making a painting.

One of the first paintings I made was a still life, oddly enough. (My mother has it at home.) When I finished it my teacher came up to me and said, "Look, I just want to tell you that the drawing in this thing is incredible," so I started working with objects. But then I started thinking that I didn't want to paint that way; I wanted to follow abstraction. So I painted a canvas that was all one color.

BR: *Your experience is different from the other artists that I know. You were encouraged by your parents to be an artist, you were encouraged by your teachers and you didn't have to go through feeling rejected. By the time you grew up, being a painter was more acceptable.*

DS: It wasn't so much that, because my father didn't think that this was going to be a good idea, but he didn't say anything about it because he had his own problems at that point. They figured that it was going to go one way or another and that everybody could do what he or she wanted. The thing about the college art department was that it was the first time I had seen adults who made a living by painting. I naturally thought that the only way you could make a living as a painter was by teaching, which didn't bother me at all.

BR: *When and where did your father take you to museums?*

DS: Everywhere we would go. We traveled and went on trips all over the place; we would drive to Florida and to different cities and in every city we would go to museums to see what they had in there. I never went to Europe with my parents, but we went to New York; wherever there was a museum, we would go. We loved to go to art shows and see what other people were doing, even sidewalk art shows, and my father never was critical; he was always looking at things and then he'd go home and do something else. I thought that was nice, because some people can be very critical. He also had a close friend at that time who was the head of the art department of the University of North Carolina at Asheville; he was a potter, so my father started throwing pots with him. This guy was a really good potter, but he was a little bit crazy. He got my father involved in the art department and my father would paint with him and they would throw pots together and hang out. My father ended up establishing a scholarship for young artists at the college. The summer of my first year in college I took off for Europe. I traveled in Greece and spent a lot of time in museums. I got very involved in Van Gogh's drawings, Seurat and Rousseau.

BR: *What is it about Rousseau that you like so much?*

DS: I don't really like him anymore. At the time I had this experience with his painting: I suddenly saw the water moving slowly in the painting of the flute player. I couldn't believe how this had happened. I began looking at how he constructed water, with alternating bands of lines, and how he had set up this perfect little environment in his painting.

BR: *There is a great degree of simplification and hard edges in the drawings which relate to yours. The construction of space, like Rousseau's, is different from traditional art.*

DS: I started drawing a lot from nature at that time. I also tried to draw old engravings to perfect technique. I would use Rembrandt's *Two Trees* or images from a magazine, like a person's head, and then try to follow the lines like an old engraving to get the volumes. I spent hours learning how to crosshatch until I realized that the way people made those lines was that they had a tool with sixteen little indentations and they could make sixteen perfectly parallel lines with one movement.

BR: *Do you think that your experience in the theater has influenced your painting in the direction of theatricality or drama?*

DS: It would have had to.

BR: *There is a kind of drama in your paintings, although it is more in the manner of a* tableau vivant *because there is no action, they are extremely static. Yet there is a kind of presentation which is almost like a proscenium; it's explicitly frontal and that is part of what painting was about at the time that you started it. Still, there is a stagelike presence to the flower paintings.*

DS: There must be something that I got from it.

BR: *And your use of light and dark value contrast was considered anti-modern when you started working.*

DS: When I was at the Art Institute in Chicago, we would always go through all of the current trends, mostly of New York art, conceptual art, video art and performance art, which was extremely important at the time. I never really liked performance art, because, coming from the theater, I saw the theater as a truer medium and thought that, as an actor, the idea was to increase the audience, not decrease it. In performance art, you were saying that you were performing for fewer and fewer people. Very few people can watch a person in a white suit walk across a ladder for very long. I felt that painting, on the other hand, was a theater in which the performance was completely visible all of the time. I felt that painting contained all of the things that were important.

BR: *At the time that you started to paint seriously there was the debate about whether theater was the enemy of art. In the late sixties, Michael Fried wrote* Art and Objecthood *and declared that theater was antithetical to the essence of painting.*

DS: I don't think that's true. People come up with these things, but they don't really have much meaning.

BR: *Do you ever think about what the essence of painting is?*

DS: No, I don't think about the essence of painting. I don't think of painting as separate from art in general. I don't think of it as something that is specialized or removed in the sense that it decreased its capacity to communicate. I don't think about painting as something to be reduced like perfume. Painting should be expanding all of the time. I come out of the period where the constrictions on it were too great.

BR: *Why are you so interested in French culture?*

DS: I studied French from the time I was in the fourth grade through college. I couldn't speak a word of it; I couldn't read it very well either. I would put on the earphones in the college language lab and I would fall asleep. So then I went to Europe and that's where I learned there was real milk in the world and real bread and things that I had never seen. I was traveling alone and I met this guy on a boat to Crete, a Québecois who I think was involved with that group of people who kidnapped the Parliamentary people in Canada; I think they killed one of them. He was on the lam and he wouldn't speak English at all. I didn't know too much about the Québecois situation, but he and I became very close to each other and we spoke French the whole time, for a month and a half. That's where I really learned to speak it and put it into practice.

BR: *Many American artists have gone to Europe. But American arrogance since the war made them extremely condescending toward Europeans.*

DS: I loved it and I loved the museums. It was the first time I had ever been to Italy. I went to Florence and I didn't have a cent. I had three hundred dollars for three months. I was through with Greece and on my way to northern Europe, and I was living on the street in Florence. I slept outdoors in the Piazza della Signoria; I slept under the *Rape of the Sabines.* When I think back on it, it was probably pretty dangerous, but it didn't seem so at that time. All the museums like the Uffizi were closed because of a strike. I just spent time wandering around the city. I'm a terrible tourist to this day; I'd rather just be in a city and walk. Unless I'm going to a museum to see things, I'm not a sightseer. The whole time I was in Europe all I did was live there and walk around. I would meet people and we would talk and eat lunch, sit in coffee shops and drink and try to be in the place.

BR: *When did you move to New York?*

DS: I moved to New York in 1975, right from graduate school at the Art Institute of Chicago. I had become friendly with Elizabeth Murray and Bob Moskowitz and Carole Squires, a photography critic. I was staying in John Torreano's loft. At that time, Richard Artschwager was moving in upstairs and he needed a crew to help, which is where I met Richard Jackson and a couple of local artists in the area. For five dollars an hour we tore down the ceilings and hauled all of the junk out. Susan and I had four hundred dollars between us and we were sharing a loft with Carole Squires. I started making money doing construction work downtown. Through Bob Moskowitz I found the loft that I am living in now; he told me that an artist named Jeff Way was moving out. That's where I met Joel Shapiro, too, because he and Allen Saret both lived in that building. Joel was moving out and Allen was moving in and I was moving in. Through Bob I met Jeff Way and he wanted a $2,500 fixture fee and the rent was $200 a month and I thought, "Oh, man, I'll never be able to afford this, but I've got to do something." So I borrowed a little money from my parents and I gave him a down payment and I told him that I would pay him the rest of the money by working for him in his new loft— hauling Sheetrock up, and doing the demolition. I worked about two months on that guy's loft to pay off the loft we were living in. That's the loft I am still in. And then I did other work like that to stay alive until I got a job working for the Denise René Gallery. I worked in the back room, shipping and hanging shows and packing stuff up. To this day I am a close friend of hers.

BR: *When did you start making a living from your work?*

DS: While I was working at her place, I was drawing and I had applied for a CAPS grant. At that time there was still such a thing as a CAPS grant. Now there are no more New York CAPS grants; they don't give money to artists anymore, which I think is a crime. That was another case of what the state does, which is find a thing that isn't broken and break it. At any rate, I got into the finals. I had dropped my slides off at Artists Space sometime after I had moved here and, at that time, Helene Weiner was running it, who is now running Metro Pictures; I had never heard anything, which you never do. Anyway, I got into the finals for the CAPS grant and I put up my work and thought that I would get some money and be able to quit my job, but I didn't get a grant that year. I was a little bit discouraged by it, but not so much. You don't expect these things to happen. I decided that taking slides around is a waste of money and I now tell people that it is one of the worst things you can possibly do. Nobody will ever do anything looking at your slides.

BR: *How does an artist get a gallery, then?*

DS: An artist has to know where he thinks his work will fit and he has to begin a dialogue with the gallery and with artists in the gallery that he respects. Know where you want to be and what you want to do and how you want your work to function in the world. It's not just a question of having a show; you can have a show and nothing will happen and that will be the end of it. You want to have a clear idea of what you want to do. Selling your art is the least of your worries, especially if you are younger, because, by and large, you've already got a job. If you are living in New York, you've got some means of supporting yourself; you've got a job and you are making your work, so what you really want to do is to make your work good and get it seen properly. Protect yourself, protect your work, don't let your things just be treated like commodities. Later on, when you are making a living from your art and everybody decides they don't want it anymore, then you have a real problem because it's hard to get a job. Stay with the job as long as possible, is what I tell them. Actually, I met most of the great people that I have dealt with through other artists that I knew and that's really how it happened. I met Paula Cooper through Richard Artschwager and I know Bob Moskowitz and Elizabeth Murray and I met Miani Johnson of Willard through different people that I knew. You gravitate toward the art you are interested in. I went to Helene Weiner, at Artists Space, and I said that I would really like to get my slides back, I don't want to leave them here anymore, and she asked me my name and I told her and she said, "Oh, I've been trying to reach you." I can't believe that anybody who says that is telling the truth because they can always reach you. And I said, "Why?" and she said, "I want to give you a show. I saw your things at the CAPS grant viewing and I love them."

BR: *What were you painting at the time?*

DS: At that time they were little paintings made of plastic and they were called "debris" paintings; they were little squares of canvas that I would pour Roplex over and I would make objects or find objects and throw them in like junk. The stuff would dry and you would have all kinds of images of debris, sort of like garbage, locked into a painting. Then I would paint some trompe l'oeil things in it. It was also manipulating the material into little primitive signs.

BR: *Did you sell those pictures?*

DS: No, I still have them.

BR: *Did anybody buy them?*

DS: No. They were only seen at that CAPS thing and then Helene said that she wanted to give me a show and I said, "Great." Then they moved into their new space—not where they are now, but over on Hudson Street. I had the first show ever in that space, but by the time they had gotten ready, I was already working with linoleum, doing the same thing.

BR: *What do you mean by doing the same thing?*

DS: That first show of those little paintings were still debris. I would take one square of black tile and I would cut out what looked

October 4, 1976 (puzzle piece).
Vinyl composite tile; 12″ x 12″.
Courtesy Blum Helman Gallery, Inc., New York.
Photo: © 1979 D. James Dee.

like animal shapes, behind the legs and the tail area. I would take it out and fit it together to make a table, put the table on the bottom and leave the parts that I had taken out on the top. Another one was a factory building in which the shapes had been cut away and laid back into a factory and a table—a lot of the images that I now use regularly but in a different way. I also did some that were larger, four by five. They were laid like parquet floors, with inlaid images: paint, bottle caps, images drawn on, cut-up saucers—stuff transmuted into other things. Helene came over and saw the first little tile pieces and she said, "I really like those little plastic things." I said, "The thing is, I'm not doing little plastic things anymore, but I want you to take a good hard look at these before you make a decision." She said, "You're right, I'll show these. I think these are pretty good." So she showed them, and for some reason it became a big, smash success, I don't know why. The press loved it and I got write-ups in *The Soho Weekly News,* which is gone now. People really liked them. This was 1977. A young woman came up to me and said, "I really want to show your work and I could really do a good job for you. Why don't you give me a chance and I'll put you in a group show? I promise you that this is going to be great." This turned out to be Mary Boone and it was in her little gallery below Leo Castelli. At the same time I had been dealing with Miani at Willard and I said to her, "Look, I really want to show here." Miani was having a lot of success with my work and she wanted to show it. I really liked Miani, too, and I liked her gallery, so I said, Why don't I do both of these things and see what happens? So I did a show with Mary and a show with Miani and things rose exponentially and I decided that I would rather be uptown since I lived in SoHo and I didn't want to be living in the area where I was showing my work.

BR: *You spoke of working in Vallauris, where Picasso made ceramics. What were you doing there?*

DS: Bob Feldman, who is still my print publisher, got the idea that, since I was working with linoleum paintings, the natural thing to do would be to make lino cuts. So we made arrangements to work with Jaime Arniera, who had done most of the lino cutting for Picasso. He had learned cutting as a prisoner of war. He really is a printer and they have a press up there. They print posters for festivals and tickets—he's not an art printer, it's just a little print shop. I didn't know this: I thought that I was going to a guy who was a linoleum printer, but he thought I was coming there to give him some drawings and he was going to trace them and he was going to do it all and he was going to do it whenever he felt like it. This wasn't what I had in mind, so I bulldozed my way into his shop, which he really hated. He was a terror. He hated this idea, even though he had agreed to it in the beginning. Finally I got some prints out.

BR: *Did you work on wood or linoleum?*

DS: Linoleum. It was a struggle to work with this material. I solved the problem by renting a house nearby that had a beautiful porch and I would leave the linoleum out in the sun and it would soften and you could cut it just like putty or clay. Arniera was horrible; he wouldn't give me any tools to work with, nothing. I finally completed a portfolio of two different sets of images which turned out quite well. They're called the "Tramp" pictures; the Museum of Modern Art has one.

BR: *What are the images?*

DS: One is a set of smokestacks and cypress trees; two cypress trees is an image and then a series of colored smokestacks. The cypresses look almost like pickles, because Italian gardeners trim them that way.

BR: *That opposition between nature and industry is the subject of so much Impressionist art. You must be aware of that?*

DS: The overriding interest I have between nature and industry is that I now look at it the way I look at figuration: from the other side. If you follow how industry and technology work historically in painting, you can watch them go from a period of great hopefulness to real awe, to where nature recedes. Now our landscape is all industrial and nature is receding. I am looking at it from growing up in the middle of it and dealing with it in the reverse. I used to think of the smokestacks as Monet's poplars; he was painting them and someone was going to buy the road and cut them down to improve it, so he had to rent the poplars and finish them before they cut them down. The concept was that these trees had become interchangeable in some way. I began to see the smokestacks like the poplars, that these things were going to go away soon too. I think of them as our forest, which is one of the reasons for the abandoned mill, the big steel mill painting at the Hirschhorn called *Plant*. It's another play on the idea that even these things are like plants.

BR: *Who ever thought there would be an artist who was nostalgic about industry?*

DS: I'm not nostalgic; I don't see it that way at all. I have no interest in it beyond the fact that it functions in a certain way and it is curious to me in painting how it relates to that function. You look at the Impressionist paintings and there is a big forest, and in the middle of it is a smokestack pumping out soot. Now I am doing smokestacks pumping out the soot, and in the middle of it you might find a little tree. But it's not nostalgic. I find it part of the landscape.

BR: *But very specifically disappearing?*

DS: In my last show I had a painting called *Rig*. If you look at all the ways that machinery has been photographed, through Charles Sheeler and all, it's incredibly abstract. Here it's gone awry and burned down. It brings an almost Expressionist point of view of line into geometry gone awry. Again, it's on the edge of being one thing and another at the same time.

BR: *Doesn't it worry you that your art is intellectual and preconceived?*

DS: I see these things after the painting is done. I make it that way as I go. Once it's done, I think I understand the painting.

BR: *How do you decide what images to use? All of the images you use appear in Impressionist painting.*

DS: I use imagery from all different kinds of things: from pre-Impressionism, American Precisionism, Expressionism. I eliminated Surrealism because I don't have that much interest in it. I find Surrealism to be a small part of a very big picture. I try to stay away from the small parts and paint the bigger picture. If you look at painting through a plane, and you think of Cubism as cracking that plane, then you can see that once that happens you can't repair the picture plane, the way you look through it or at art. We can't see any paintings without looking through that point in history. People have a longing for things that are gone, nostalgia, for example, or sentimentality. If you don't have access to those things immediately—which you don't, after Cubism—you can't look at classical art or even at Piero della Francesca without also thinking of Cubism. What happens is that all you have of the past in cultures is a memory, which is not your memory anyway because you weren't there.

BR: *There is an effort to preserve whatever is still viable, or transform it into something that is relevant and viable.*

DS: What do you mean "transform"?

BR: *I see that as being part of the intention of the work, to try to conserve as much of the tradition of painting as remains viable.*

DS: I don't think that's true. I am not involved in conserving the tradition. I don't have any interest in that so much as an interest in going with all of this history forward in terms of painting.

BR: *That painting* Rig *has relief that is more pronounced than in most of your work.*

DS: *London* was even more pronounced; it has huge elements left on, almost baroque.

BR: *How did you develop your concept of space and of creating a space that is post-Cubist?*

DS: By looking hard at how people have approached space at all different times. Most of the time when a person is drawing or painting they keep trying to eliminate the "them" from it and make it merge with something outside of them. The point is that you have to learn to accept the "you" in your work. Once I did that, it didn't matter what I painted because whatever I painted would be modern. I stopped worrying about what to paint and started painting whatever was around. That developed into the imagery that I use now. I had no interest in narrative painting, illusionistic painting or being totally flat. I had no interest in being totally abstract, I had no interest in being figurative. I wanted to combine these things somehow to create a viable situation that both had power and meaning and was riddled with kinds of para-doxes that feed on each other so they can have a life. I started looking at Rembrandt's self-portraits and how he punched his hands through the picture plane—how he literally had his hands out in front of the picture—and how other people had used the space behind to make that world like a window that you could enter through. How they shaped volume and how when one looked at a monochrome Robert Ryman or a flat painting, there was space inherent in it. I felt that if I could combine these things, if I could make the painting surface function in all the ways that it can function—the ways it can go in and out, around, behind, thin, thick, all of these things at once—then I would have accomplished something. I am still working on this concept. That's why you have the edges of the paintings removed from the stretcher bars—so that you can see behind and through the painting, but also to show that everything, from the back up, is standard manufactured art material. I wanted to emphasize that this is painting; it's not about sculpture or process. Building up the edges with plywood was all about gluing, veneers, surfaces, all the way up to the front of the picture, which would then have this skin that you could fall back into. You had something going out and something going in at the same time inherent in just the structure. Then you worked on top of that with something else.

BR: *Illusionism becomes tenable in modernist painting as long as it is revealed as being illusion or contradicted to the point where it cannot convince you that you are looking at something real. You found a new way of doing that. You talked about the method of creating space, using larger and smaller elements and their relationships and the use of perspective as contradictions by reversing the convention of creating our sense of distance by putting smaller elements in the foreground. Why did you take the space created in traditional paintings, subvert it and turn it inside out?*

DS: I was working with generic imagery and had built out to using a standard three-point perspective to create space.

BR: *Did you study perspective?*

DS: No, but I got a book when I became involved in creating a space out of repetition of images. The first spatial one I did might have been *Rain*. With figures, unless you are painting dwarves, if there's a little person back here and a big person up close, you know that that little person is in the distance. If you do that with something else in which scale is subverted—like a cypress tree—then all cypress trees look pretty much the same whether they are big or little. Perspective can function as spatial recession and still

Rain July 8, 1982.
Oil, charcoal and encaustic on tile over wood; 96″ x 48″.
Courtesy Blum Helman Gallery, Inc., New York.
Photo: Courtesy Blum Helman Gallery, Inc., New York.

look flat. That's the way in which I first started thinking about perspective. If you use something like a lamppost and it goes back in receding perspective, you get the depth. But if you take people close up and you have one taller than the other, either you have a short person and a tall person, or one is in front and one is in back. If you put people adjacent like that and moosh them together along with these other perspective lines, you get a strange interplay, especially if you don't have definition or distinctions. I eliminated all features and all of the little things in between the bodies that would allow you to determine their relationship to one another.

BR: *Why do you create that swing back and forth between flatness and depth—which also happens with your imagery where it can be read as abstract or imagistic, where it rides the line between representation and abstraction because the images are so generalized (you call them generic)? Why do you like that line?*

DS: It seems like the place to be. That seems to be the only way to continue and take all the elements from one side and all the things that were unknown on the other side and put them together in a genuine way and see if you couldn't haul painting into the twenty-first century. You have to find a way to do that because otherwise it's going to be irrelevant.

BR: *There is an attempt in a large part of your work to express the contradictory nature of our contemporary experience. It's not a reflection of social or political events, but of a psychological state that has to do with paradox, ambiguity, reversals: things seeming to be one thing and potentially being something else.*

DS: The human mind does not really want to accept that; mostly, what they see is a lie. That's exactly where we are living now, in the sense that everything you basically look at is a lie. The mind does not want to accept this, so you believe that when you look at a magazine that people actually look this way. People go to spas thinking that this can happen, when what they are trying to do is a lie to begin with. The mind does not want to accept reality as a complete lie. They try to mold the lie into a reality again, which is impossible to do.

BR: *That's part of living in a technological media civilization where these lies are created for consumption, in order to seduce people into buying things.*

DS: It's more complex than that, because it's compromised completely down the line. As you get more and more removed from reality, it's more and more difficult to function. People want painting more now. That's temporary, because eventually, if there's enough pressure on it, the painting will all begin to tell the same lies. If that continues to happen, painting in America will go the way that movies have gone. I can't watch most movies. I think that the first example of deliberate manipulation was Lauren Bacall singing "How Little We Know"—and it was Andy Williams's voice! People who want to be actors in the movies are horrified when I say that you don't have to be an actor. A good director and editor can make anybody do whatever they want for the part. People look at painting, these goofy little things, and think there is some truth revealed there—and there is. There is some truth revealed there, because it is a real thing. The explosion in the eighties was all about throwing up as much stuff between the viewer and the art as you possibly could to obscure the experience of the work: the hoopla, the lighting, the gallery, the architecture, the fashion. Right away it's, "Here's my painter, this is my artist, this is his work, but you've got to buy it quick, come back here." People in gallery worlds have come to the conclusion that painting can be a mass medium, which it isn't.

BR: *Is the visible grid pattern that is created by using tiles a reference to the Cubist grid or to Mondrian's grid?*

DS: No, the grid comes out of the minimalist aesthetic of using manufactured materials and repetition. Those were the materials available, and when I put them up it seemed very logical that I should have been so impressed by Carl Andre's sculptures. When I began painting conscious works in about 1969, I'd be painting on the floor; then when I went to the painting studios and schools, I started painting on canvases on the floor. You would stretch it out on the floor and work on it like Pollock did. Since the canvases were big you would work down with big paint so you could be in the middle of it. It made perfect sense to me to simply pick up the floor. Then I started seeing what I had been absorbing. It wasn't that I intended to do that, that's the way it ended up.

BR: *You don't deny that anything in minimal art happened. There is an acknowledgment that pop art brought back the image; it created a kind of post–Abstract Expressionist style and at the same time there were elements taken from minimalism: the work is not pop, it's not minimal. I've always defined true innovation as the synthesis of everything that preceded the point at which you enter into the dialogue.*

DS: Looking at art in general and respecting the achievements of people before you is the least that you can do.

BR: *That everything is remembered, that there is such a thing as historical memory is a moral statement at this point, because one of our fundamental moral problems has to do with memory. We don't build with prior knowledge.*

DS: Would you say that with no memory there is no God? It's an interesting idea.

BR: *I don't know. Do you believe in God?*

DS: I don't know, but I think that it's something to think about. If there is no memory, how can one even think of anything sublime? What is the sublime?

BR: *It's the intuition of the miraculous.*

DS: Without memory, how can one have that?

BR: *You also cannot have morality.*

DS: You can make the statement that without memory there is no God and if you can't deal with that concept, how can you make art or bother doing anything? You might as well watch TV all day.

BR: *Television is constantly shortening the attention span, breaking it up into smaller and smaller units. It destroys the capacity for continuity or for thinking about anything for a long time. Complex issues take concentration and continuity. Why do you work on one picture for so long?*

DS: I find that the longer you take, the better things get because it leaves you more time to think and to work with and learn from what you are doing while you are doing it. There is a moment when every quick act makes the thing work and is the art. But while you are getting to the moment, there are so many areas in which you want to change something or you see something that you want to add.

BR: *You say that you think a lot about Pollock. I see in the way you work paintings in which he cut out of the web to create shapes that were not depicted, but part of the background which was removed. The idea that painting is dead became popular because there was no one around intelligent enough to learn from Pollock and go beyond his crisis in reconciling figuration with post-Cubist space.*

DS: I talked earlier about Cubism and cracking and breaking the glass of the picture plane, and that looking back now at other paintings it is impossible not to have Cubism in your mind. Pollock totally shattered the glass. I'm not just talking about the picture plane, but the ways of looking through paintings. Once again, I think that these changes are permanent, you don't go on and forget about it. Cubism was permanent, chiaroscuro was permanent, the Renaissance perspective was permanent, Pollock is permanent: these are permanent things, so you are looking at history and a dialectic.

BR: *The development in your work is evolutionary; it doesn't jump around. It's always coming out of itself and tending toward greater complexity. In the new work there is elaborate detail. To have that much detail is to contradict the premise of the color-field painters, where there is no detail.*

You work in a way definable as dialectical materialism. There is a great concern with the material object and with the production of material objects, which one would identify as a Marxist concern.

DS: Part of that is thinking about painting as a work, or work. I don't like that, but I can't escape it.

BR: *Even though your works are static and they don't deal with the element of time and narration, nevertheless you feel the amount of time that has gone into making this object: you know that somebody didn't do it in three hours. That's part of the content of the work.*

The first thing you see in your work is the image, which is single. Even in the "disaster" paintings, which are scenes, it still is a surface divided.

DS: Do you remember the railroad track painting in the last show called *Switching Signals?* That was a painting that I had been wanting to make for years and didn't know quite how to do. It was like a snapshot that you take of the landscape when you are up on a mountain and it looks so great, and when you get it developed you have a picture of nothing. I wanted to make a painting that was a picture of nothing and I think that that does it. You look at it and there is nothing, but yet it is something else. That took the abstract about as far as I could go. That painting was a view of the railroad track for the Washington corridor showing the switching

SWITCHING SIGNALS MAY 29, 1987.
Tar and latex on tile over Masonite; 96″ x 96¾″.
Courtesy Blum Helman Gallery, Inc., New York.
Photo: Sheldon Collins.

signals after that train crash. They had taken a snapshot of the switching signals down the track and they presented this as an image, and it was a picture of nothing! Of course, it turned out that the engineer had been coked up and just ran into something.

BR: *There are two categories of your images: one is still life, either fruit or flowers, and the other is landscape.*

DS: That's about it.

BR: *There is not much ambiguity in the still-life pictures; they are very much about the image and process. But the landscape paintings are very multivalent; they open to all kinds of interpretations, sometimes conflicting interpretations, just as you said. For some people, the notion of the railroad brings to mind the memories of that image of the railroad to Auschwitz. You separate those two categories in a disorienting way.*

DS: One of the things that makes that railroad to Auschwitz so frightening is that in order to move all those people, one had to be so removed from the act of what was going on that they simply made it a system, a process. I get involved with it in these paintings too; that process, by itself, is also dangerous.

BR: *That's what I was trying to say. It is not so much dangerous as meaningless. If you have no goals and you have no objectives, you are in the free-floating environment in which we live.*

DS: That's why it is so incredible when people say, "He's denying truth to materials."

BR: *What does that mean?*

DS: It doesn't mean anything. People misunderstand the words "truth to materials." I don't believe there is any truth to materials. Materials have integrity, but that is a different thing. I'm not trying to trick you into thinking that this is something else or that I am trying to hide what it is. It's not about that at all. On the other hand, even if I were doing that—that would be interesting.

BR: *You have a tremendous awareness of media—you've worked with media, you take photographs—the images may even be based on photographs, but then, so were Degas's and Bonnard's (and it turns out that virtually everybody in the nineteenth century after the invention of photography used it). Nevertheless, I don't have the sense that I'm looking through a media image when I see a painting of yours. If there is a kind of simplification, it's more on the order of how Courbet or Manet used the* images d'Épinal *as a kind of shorthand way of communicating figuration—just the opposite of all these painters who get their images by projecting slides onto the canvas and tracing them.*

DS: I thought of that, too, at one point. I was having a hell of a time drawing something. I rented this overhead thing and I projected it up on the canvas and I looked at it and I thought, "You know, if I do that, it's going to look like a photograph." It would also eliminate the decision-making of my drawing that makes the work function. So I just turned the light off and went back to drawing it myself. You know you always make it bigger or smaller or whatever, and you end up with a picture that's different. Looking at a photo and working from it, I don't take the grids and grid it off; I don't want it to be accurate. I'll just fit enough of the image in to make it work. So I lose the photograph at a certain point.

BR: *There's a great awareness in your work of the framing edge and the formal qualities of painting.*

DS: I think that's now second nature to me. I don't consciously think of it that way.

BR: *It seems that certain moments in art history are decisive. When, for example, instead of depicting an image on a ground, Barnett Newman divided the field, you could no longer compose in the old way.*

DS: In fact, in a number of pictures of mine that I did a few years ago, I used a telephone pole or a light pole to divide the picture, like Newman, to separate it—not to make a space but just to function as a bar across the two planes. I would use it a little more askew. I want everything in the paintings to be slightly askew.

BR: *Why?*

DS: Because I think that things are slightly askew anyway! I think it's the way I see things. I noticed that when Philip Johnson's building went up, the big AT&T building, it was this incredible marble stuff. I would drive by it and I would see that they had these incredibly ornate planters with trees in front of them, and they were all crooked—they just plopped them in! That's the way the thing is, you can't worry whether or not it *looks* that way, or it *should* look that way. People say, "Don't you find that your work is too beautiful?" Well, I don't care about these issues. It ends up the way it ends up.

BR: *What do you care about?*

DS: I want the painting to work. I want it to do what I want it to do and I want it to say to me that it's right. And if somebody says, "That's too beautiful," well, then, go get another painting. You don't want to mess it up just to make it look acceptable. If it turns out to look great that way, well, fine. If it doesn't, fine. Some things that I have made don't have any relationship to what you would classically think of as beautiful. If you can make something beautiful out of that goop, why not? I don't worry about these things that much. There's so much stuff out there, I don't worry about aesthetic issues.

BR: *Certain categories, for various reasons, become taboo. The category of the decorative, for example. To make decorative art, to say something's decorative art is pejorative.*

DS: I agree with that.

BR: *It wasn't always. In the eighteenth century it was the greatest thing you could say about somebody.*

DS: I think they've always had this problem of the decoration; even among the Greeks, other painters used to think the still-life painters sucked. In fact, there's no painting muse, you know!

BR: *Still life was always considered the lowest category. It's interesting that you would choose it for a large part of your work. You do still lifes and landscapes, history paintings, but not portraits.*

DS: I haven't done portraits yet, although I've made portraits through the Polaroid, snapshots. That's about it. When I saw Chuck Close's big heads in 1965, I said, "This is the truth of figure painting. This is it. This is as good as it gets, this guy has done it, forget about it." Snapshot portrait is where it's at in portraiture, period.

BR: *That would explain why you don't use it as an image.*

DS: People have been telling me, "You should do it, you should do it." I think strategically I should have made some little portraits of people. But I'm not interested in strategy in painting anyway. It's just not an interesting thing for me. I think that you just keep opening up doors. I haven't figured out a way to make a meaningful portrait. If I do, I will do it. I went to a show of drawings from the Albertina. I saw this drawing of a young prince and it practically blew me out of the room and I thought, What would be the point if I can't make a portrait that has this kind of power to it?

BR: *You refer constantly to power. It's obviously your intention to make the work powerful. Why is it necessary?*

DS: Paintings can change your life. They have mine, and I'm sure other people's too. What is painting but a medium of the mind?

BR: *A lot of dumb people do it.*

DS: If you're really good, then you're really not that dumb. If you're really that dumb, you're really not that good.

But they used to say about Léger that *les peintres sont bêtes*—"painters are dumb." At a certain point it was thought that artists were stupid. It wasn't thought so before because they had contact with philosophers. If the mind can make something that has a power outside of itself, it can exude that without the person there explaining it. That's what you really want from a work of art: you want to be surprised by it all the time. You want it to have enough dialogue to carry on a prolonged conversation past your lifetime. It's like a booster rocket; it has to contain that fire. And it takes a lot out of a person to put it in there. I don't like the idea of diddling around. I don't think of this as a cottage industry. I don't think of craft; I have no interest in these things. In order to be rigorous with yourself, you have to take brickbats. You have to try things. When people are going one way, you have to take a hard look and see whether or not that has to do with anything. In the late seventies, beginning of the eighties, I remember people screaming "The sixties are back! The sixties are back!" The sixties are not back, nothing is back. Nothing ever comes back.

BR: *When I see op art now, being done again as "neo-geo," it makes me crazy. It was bad enough the first time.*

DS: I gave up being an entertainer. It's my life; I don't think that it should be easy for people to like it. The dialogue between art and the public is what makes it work, but when you're doing it you don't think of the other people. You have to think that there has to be some relationship between you and something else. You go on a blind leap of faith that this will have some meaning aside from its meaning to you. Although that's not always the case!

49

BR: I believe in divine inspiration. That's another unpopular thing I say. I think that some people have a gift and a message.

DS: I don't know why they can't accept that in painting. They accept it in music, they accept it in running, they accept it in every other field: "This guy can do something you can't do." But with painting they look at it and say, "Anybody can do that."

BR: We live in a quantity situation creating mass marketing demand.

DS: I'm not against any of these ideas. I just think that people are looking every day in the face of complete fabrication and the mind does not want to accept it. For example, take the experience of these little Polaroids that I'm blowing up through laser technology. There are only two places in New York where they can do this; they may be the only places in the United States. What they mainly do is advertising and magazines. It's all done on computer screens. I went up there and I'm looking at this picture that they've blown up—it's a woman in a T-shirt ad—and they blow up a section of it on a computer screen and they take a little cursor and use it like an airbrush, only it goes into the facets. So what they do is they take out all the wrinkles. If she has a bad arm, they shape it. By the time you're through you have a perfect-looking thing. They had a guy and girl lying down in striped bathing suits. They didn't like the fact that the guy had hair on his body, so they eliminated the hair. They didn't like his belly button, so they changed that to a little mark. And they didn't like the fact that the bathing suit wrinkled around his cock, but they wanted the cock, for obvious reasons. So they made the line around it darker and eliminated the wrinkles, and then they made all of the lines on their bathing suits perfectly straight. They shaped the girl's leg so it was perfect, eliminated all the glare off her skin, any skin tone whatsoever. And this was the ad that went out. And people are thinking, "God, this girl has a beautiful body." There's no body like that.

BR: *Look what happened to Elvis Presley. They make pop stars into icons of a cult. That's what Andy Warhol was essentially commenting on. There seems to be no way out of it, because by making himself into one of those icons, he himself became subject to that process of depersonalization.*

DS: People don't realize that the contemporary art scene is run by Warholians and they are being victimized by it.

BR: *Warhol's influence was immense and, I think, negative. It's like Duchamp. Duchamp's influence has been, by and large, anticreative and negative. He himself admits that in the way he structures the* Last Piece *in Philadelphia, where only one person at a time can see it.*

DS: Media is a one-way communication. There is no conversation. I think that artists are deluding themselves into believing that this is the future and that's where we're really headed. I think they're completely wrong. I think they're going to find that out when somebody comes into their place and hits them over the head with an ax and that's going to be the end of it. You have to pay attention; you have to have some level of reality. I realize also that as an artist gets successful, and as he gets more and more used to comforts—and I'm guilty of this—he loses contact with reality. If you're going to stay in touch, you have to make an effort to do it. I really haven't done as much as I should—and it's not going out to nightclubs, either.

BR: *What would it be?*

DS: I don't know yet. I'm working on that like I'm working on portraiture. I can see that if I were to continue to live this way, as I got older I would become irrelevant. You have to have contact with reality, and I'm not quite sure what that is.

BR: *I think it's the nature of the human condition and very few people understand what that is at this point.*

DS: I think that's true, they don't. I don't. But I know that it's easy to lose contact; it's easy to isolate yourself from it. I don't think it has to do with being rich; it has to do with getting more and more into your own work to the exclusion of what it is that makes you want to make work to begin with. I had this dream once where I was being interviewed and they asked me, "What's the hardest part about being an artist?" I said that there were two hard things about being an artist. One is that when you're young and you're all fired up and you're working, the hard thing is to keep the "you" in your art and make the work actually be relevant and strong and true. That's the first hard thing. And when you get to that·point and people participate in your enterprise and begin to flatter you and tell you how fabulous you are, don't believe it. And the second thing is, as you get older, you must stay relevant because you become more and more isolated in your own cocoon with your ideas and your work. You get further and further out, like a mad scientist, and pretty soon you're developing things that have no meaning whatsoever. So there were two hard things to do: to be good to begin with and then to stay good. That's the trick. The hardest thing would have to be staying good.

BR: And then there's the problem of "no second acts in American lives." There's only one act, that's youth, and after that there's never maturity.

DS: I don't believe that. If I have to live somewhere else to do it, I will.

BR: That's the thing about Europe—it's more grown up, it's older, they've been through more. The only war we fought here was against each other.

DS: There are lots of things I don't like about Europe. I don't like that they hate Jews. I don't like the class structure that every country has. If you're there long enough, you realize why people came out of there. I don't have this great longing for Europe in that sense. I like Europe for other things.

BR: *Why do you like Europe? Why do you spend summers in France?*

DS: I like Europe, especially France, because I like the self-possession of the people. I like their ability to have an inner life. To be insular they have a self-possession that could really only come from a rigid structure. I like that about them, but the way in which they achieved that, the sameness, the trendiness, the slavish devotion to one thing, the acceptance of things that we don't accept, their hatreds and jealousies and rivalries, I don't share.

BR: *But we have a very rigid class structure, except that it's constantly mutating because it's based on money.*

DS: I'm not that optimistic—I'm not mad about some of those things, some of them make your hair stand on end—but I am saying that I don't go into Europe blind, either. The funny thing is, everything is getting so specialized that you're going to have Foodland in France, maybe Bookland. You're going to have Theaterland and Movieland in England, you're going to have Cultureland in Italy, and you're going to have Musicland in America, or Videoland. You're going to have all these little countries that can do one thing. That is the most frightening thing of all.

BR: *This country, which should have been progressing in terms of its sensibilities and tastes, hasn't. There are only the surface accoutrements of designer clothes and Italian furniture and gourmet food.*

DS: It's amazing, you can't even get real bread. And my hometown, Asheville, North Carolina, now is basically a giant hospital. They've got banks and hospitals and they haven't got anything else left. Every school I ever went to, as soon as I left it, was either demolished or changed. My grammar school was knocked down, my junior high school was razed, my boarding school merged, went co-op and changed its name.

BR: *Tell me about the Polaroids you take.*

DS: I've taken simple Polaroid portraits of people on the porch in St.-Tropez, always in the same place, sometimes the side varies, but always on the porch. The reason the spot looks so good is that [Paul] Signac used the porch; it overlooks the garden. All the surfaces are different-colored, so as the light moves across, you get incredible variations of light. I think he must have painted it that way and they have kept it pretty much the same. I don't know why he did that; maybe it was just a haphazard painting.

BR: *Signac never did anything except for a reason. He was constantly experimenting with color and light and he was doing it scientifically, for a purpose.*

DS: After taking Polaroid portraits of people who visit the house, I felt that the size was too small, and since there was only the original, I decided that I should enlarge them. Just in the act of trying to enlarge an SX-70 accurately, I ended up calling all over the world and finding the one place—in New York (they have one in Germany, too)—that has a system that could do this. I sent the stuff up there, they sent the things back and it was going great until I decided that I was having trouble reproducing one the way I wanted it. So I went up there to see them and found myself in this place that looks like—it's just beautiful—it's a very stylish and high-tech computer-laser reproduction system. It was so odd that, doing the most simple thing, I would find myself at kind of the cutting edge of high technology and the farthest-out ways of doing it.

One of the reasons that I began being interested in going up there was that the laser people had intimated that they could take a color Polaroid SX-70 and reproduce it in black and white. I didn't know that they could do that. I had been thinking of taking some industrial landscapes for myself, but I wanted them to be black and white and I wanted them to be Polaroid; I wanted them to be my normal way of working for studies.

BR: *The Polaroid does give you a somewhat fuzzy image, and your industrial landscapes are, opposed to your flowers or fruit, more painterly and* malerisch: *there are no hard contours, whereas in the still lifes there are.*

DS: I decided that perhaps I should try it, and also I found out that they can take a section of the Polaroid and make a picture of it. I had more control now over that little square than I had thought before, and maybe I can have a new way of working with photography that I can use in the paintings. The point is that even doing the simplest things, you come out with a completely new way of looking at something. Your work leads you into these things. You don't think up new ideas, they are revealed to you in some way.

BR: *Any artist has crises, but the way in which you represent yourself, you don't have these crises. Psychological crisis does not seem to be a part of your life.*

DS: But everybody develops their art according to their life, and that is something they have to work with. You use what you have.

BR: *Artists stop working for periods of time because they get crazy and then they get it back together again.*

DS: But their work is a result of that. I'm a different kind of person. I have all the complex relationships that children of the middle class have; on the one hand you want to be crazy, but on the other hand you're not.

BR: *Who wants to be crazy?*

DS: I don't mean crazy in the sense of out of control, but you want to get that extreme exhilaration or intense highs. What's that Southern a capella song—"You never do want what you have got, you always want what you done give away." You are always looking to do something outside of yourself. You always want to be slightly different, or you want to experience in some different way. And you do with what you have; you are always going to be the person you are. Being an artist and a child of the American middle class, you are torn between the rigorous intellectual life that you want and the feelings of also wanting to belong to the people who work with their hands—thinking of painting as a job to do, and on the other side thinking that it isn't really a job, and on the one hand organizing it like a nine to five job, but on the other hand knowing that in that nine to five you can lie down and go to sleep.

BR: *That's a problem that starts with your generation. It wasn't like that before.*

DS: The Abstract Expressionists had other problems, first of all of painting and not being able to reconcile being successful and being outsiders. We all have a dichotomy between the ways we think of our work and our lives. You always have the battle between the chaotic parts of your nature and the more controlled parts. When any one of those things dominates, the proper work isn't going to be done.

BR: *I haven't noticed much chaos breaking out in you.*

DS: I can't say what the future will bring, but extremely chaotic or theatrical gestures are not enough now to produce any work of real meaning. A totally intellectual, ideological approach is not going to produce work of any meaning. Somehow now the dialectic between those chaotic things and those desires for order has to be combined to put together a new framework of looking at painting. Once that happens, who knows what will happen next?

BR: *You sound very much like a Post-Impressionist critique of Impressionism.*

DS: Post-Impressionists touched on using more scientific methods. I'm not sure they consist of more than three people.

BR: *It consists of a lot more than that, but maybe three good people.*

DS: I was standing in front of *La Grand Jatte* in Chicago with Ian Dunlop and I said, "I think that in this Seurat, the drawing is very awkward," and that the rigorous and obsessive quality actually produced, except in a couple of works, is stiff work. But on the other hand you have to say, Not bad for twenty-seven years old. He died when he was thirty-two.

BR: *The labor of making* La Grande Jatte *is very obvious. It's such a labored picture; it lacks the grace of* The Bathers.

DS: The problem is that with the way America is rolling along, we are going to make *La Grande Jatte* the same thing as the Rousseau moon painting—a kind of charming backdrop of some kind of *naif,* which it certainly wasn't. I think it would be great to see a major Seurat exhibition. That would be fabulous. His drawings alone have influenced almost everybody.

BR: *Have they influenced you?*

DS: I think they have.

BR: *There is a special relationship between the graininess of the paper and the absence of hard outlines in the drawings, the softness of the drawings and the blacks.*

DS: Part of the great genius of Seurat was the drawings. I think that's also true of Van Gogh. Johns's early gray drawings have

Seurat's influence. Seurat has influenced almost everybody who has seriously thought about drawing, because he was one of the first to actually take the paper into account.

BR: *Why are we in a period in which "artists" have no respect for art?*

DS: It's a heavy load to carry, so it's a way of absolving yourself of responsibility. But that is also a sign of the times we are living in, where nobody is responsible, or will accept responsibility for anything. That's why X kills Y—it's really a tragedy, or that's what a tragedy is: two lives have been ruined. But X accepts no responsibility for it and we can't agree that so-and-so should pay for this.

BR: *But you told me that you don't feel guilt. Where is responsibility without guilt?*

DS: I don't think that guilt has anything to do with responsibility. You can accept responsibility for your actions and not feel guilty about them. People tell you how horrible they are but you don't see it that way.

BR: *There's a definite decision on your part to limit the number of motifs and to recycle those motifs, to reuse them. Why? And how do you choose the motifs?*

DS: I'm not locked into it. If I can be spun into another motif, I'll do it.

BR: *You did describe how the tulips became lemons, how they spawned, in a sense, another generation of images.*

DS: The tulips came from the smokestacks and fires.

BR: *And how now the lemons are becoming eggs. Why do you use what you refer to as generic images?*

DS: It's a holdover from trying to work with generic materials and objects. It eliminates a lot of decisions that I don't feel are necessary to make. For example, I decided to work on the squares in degrees of standard, repetitive forms because I couldn't really understand why one would choose one size canvas over another size canvas. Why would you pick a four-by-six or a six-by-eight? Why would you decide a vertical was more interesting than a horizontal and how long should the horizontal be? These all seemed to be aesthetic decisions and I didn't want to make those decisions. I felt they could be eliminated from truly modern painting. So I picked these images that would evolve out of each other in an exponential range. Because I'm following that tenet now doesn't mean that I won't change it.

BR: *Your images are so generalized. Do you feel that they have any kind of connotative content? Do they create associations that are understood in some way? You don't necessarily think about fruit and flowers when you look at them.*

DS: No, and that's not the point. With the cigarettes and the smoke, you don't really think of the smoke or the cigarette so much. The flowers . . . look at this red carnation—there's no variation in it. And yet there's something machinelike, too, so that all of these things tend to conform to a standard or generic idea. I use flowers because they give a range that the other images don't give, because I can be free with those in a way that I can't be with the fruits in that they're formless. A flower can be formless. Fruits are volumetric, and the landscapes can be both formless and volumetric. Of course they can also have illusions, and I don't want to give up any of these things. Given that range, I find that it keeps expanding. If I think of something else, or they reveal something else that I should consider, I am happy to do it. Maybe I am locked into a certain dogma, but I am open to having it changed if I think it needs to be changed. I am involved in a repetitive process of working. I decided to eliminate color choices. For example, I don't mix paint and I don't mix colors.

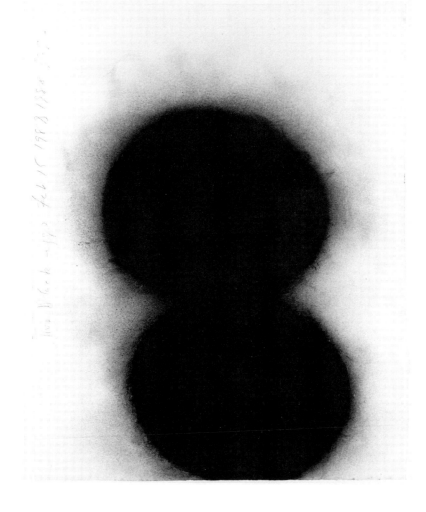

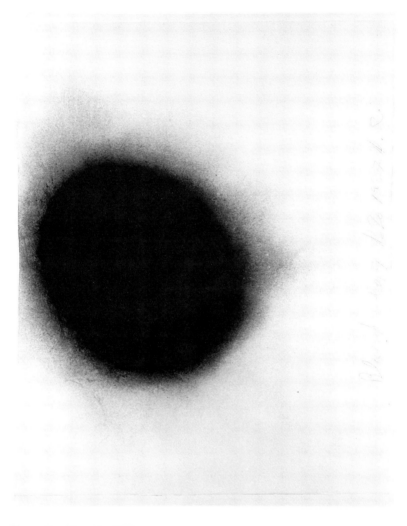

Black Egg Dec. 20, 1987.
Charcoal on paper; 60″ x 48″.
Courtesy Blum Helman Gallery, Inc., New York.
Photo: Pelka/Noble Photography.

Two Black Eggs Feb. 15, 1988.
Charcoal on paper; 60″ x 48″.
Courtesy Blum Helman Gallery, Inc., New York.
Photo: Pelka/Noble Photography.

BR: *This is a very Johnsian way of working, of making a set of decisions.*

DS: Not just Johns, it's probably true of other people.

BR: *In Johns there is an idea that painting is a language. He was going to identify the units of that language and then recombine and alter them. There were a set number of motifs that he would claim as his and then he would use the spectrum colors. The line between image and abstraction, to have something vacillate back and forth, you first find it in his work.*

DS: What about De Kooning's women?

BR: *I don't see it there.*

DS: You don't see those women being abstract and figurative?

BR: *No, I see them as figurative paintings.*

DS: I'd like to go on the record as saying purely abstract painting is a relatively small block in the history of art. Pure abstract painting without imagery is a very small period in art history and it's about to come to a close. It will reappear but in a different guise.

BR: *The interesting artists are going back to the sources.*

DS: They are going to have to go back through us, through abstract image painting in order to make another kind of abstraction. They are going to have to deal with it. Somebody *will* do it, then abstract painting will have another life again.

BR: *You also said something that I think is key, about the paintings with lemons and the prints of drawings related to them, that they had a kind of erotic content. Anyone can respond to that—anyone will respond to that; you don't have to know anything about art.*

DS: One of the things painting can't do very well is to shock you with literal inhumanity. It doesn't save the world; it doesn't teach people how brutal people are to each other. Even in Goya's war paintings, what we get are his feelings about the kinds of horrors and superstitions you see there, but Goya didn't have to literally write down that they bit their genitals off and so forth. Other media do that better. That's not to say that one should abrogate his responsibility, but you can trivialize things so easily.

BR: *Who are the artists that you most admire?*

DS: I could preface that by eliminating all of the clichés, people like Cézanne, Pollock—all of the people that you *have* to admire because you really can't avoid it and must take it as a given—and get into the more quirky ones that I admire. Then I can talk about Sassetta, who has meant an awful lot to me.

BR: *Why?*

DS: Because it's another one of those rare occasions in which you see a guy struggling, coming out of iconic art trying to make a narrative. I love the way the paintings work, in which the same guy reappears big and little, and it's because he's moved from one place to another. They are true paintings. You can tell a good artist from a bad artist because the good artists mean what they say and the other ones don't. Skipping the obvious great Italians, I like Petrus Cristus and some of the Northern works, Van Eyck. Paintings on such a small scale contain so much information and can be so powerful, the obvious thing being the mirror and the reflections and the concepts of perception, and also his invention of oil paint. He was inventing materials as he went along. In addition to that, I consider Van Eyck to be one of the first serious still-life painters, even though he used portraiture. They are really set up like still lifes and he is beginning to abstract, even though they are so focused. Somebody once said that you can really tell that an artist like Zurbarán was cranking out paintings and I say,

Try to crank out paintings with a 00 brush. It isn't easy to do. Van Eyck was almost more a technician than an artist, but what a great technician!

BR: *Why do you paint small paintings?*

DS: I started using the one square unit of tile as a canvas. I've always done small paintings, the canyons between buildings and puzzle pieces and so forth. I used the small ones as a way of manipulating ideas more easily. At the time I was doing the "factory" paintings, I started thinking about the cigarette and human architecture. So the first cigarette paintings were small because, at that time, I thought that I would make the larger architectural images larger. All of those pictures are inset in a sort of half frame; they were about looking at architecture through a window, being enclosed, being in New York and always looking out the window at things. With cigarettes, I thought that I would make them cigarette size. I make these little human-size architectural pictures. Then when I moved into the still lifes, I started using it as a way of working with scale, as a way of saying that large scale is within the scale of the frame. Then I could make as powerful a small painting as most people make large ones. At the time I started doing them people thought that important works could only be done on a giant scale.

BR: *That's the "heroism" of the New York School.*

DS: Heroism does not have anything to do with the size of a canvas.

BR: *What's your idea of heroism?*

DS: The definition of a hero is a person who acts in a selfless way for the benefit of somebody else, risking his life to do it at all costs. People don't set out to be heroic; they find themselves in those situations and act instinctively. The person who pulls somebody out from under a train is acting heroically.

BR: *Why have we lost the concept of heroism? We live in a culture that has no concept of the heroic act. It is very hard to make ambitious art.*

DS: It goes against the grain of heroism in the first place to think only of yourself. People misunderstand heroism. Promoting yourself over others is not a heroic act.

BR: *One of the problems of American culture is that we had heroic figures. Whether they merited it, people did conceive of the Kennedys as heroic. Martin Luther King, Jr., certainly was heroic. And they got killed. In a way, the message is if you want to be a hero, you want to be dead. That has had an effect, not only the demoralization of young people in general and stopping protest, but it has also had an extremely negative effect on art.*

DS: That's true. I would never say that I am a hero.

BR: *On the other hand, maintaining a stance of opposition in the face of intense totalitarian pressure to conform, that is heroic.*

DS: No, that's called character and having character. Character is as important as heroism. Heroism, by and large, is usually accidental. I certainly wouldn't want to discourage people from doing that. New York tends to discourage heroic behavior.

BR: *Well, if you are living with rats in a behavioral sink . . . we know what happens to them in those environmental conditions: they turn on each other.*

DS: If you talk about classic heroes, they didn't see an alternative. It's not that they wanted to be shot at or wanted to risk their lives, they had to do it.

You always feel that if there are people on the street, there's a certain amount of safety, but there really isn't. And if we can't be protected from each other, if we are living in fear of each other, what kind of a life is it? It's a terrible way to live.

BR: *Bill Rubin said something that always stuck with me, which is that we are the first people to be conscious of our own decline. The question is whether this is reversible. Is this the American destiny—do we really have to end up like this? Or is it just an episode, just a rerun of the Gilded Age that will go away and be supplanted by something better? That leads us to another problem, which is the debasement of language. Look at the debasement in this country of the English language. Neologisms are spawned every five seconds. Did you know that the new verb is "to Fed-Ex"? "I'll Fed-Ex that to you tomorrow"?*

DS: Really?

BR: *And the verb "to office"? "I'm officed in the such-and-such"?*

DS: To office? It's a verb?

BR: *The worst is the perverse use of language to say something that actually means the opposite or to mouth platitudes that don't apply to the situation that you are talking about. It's again a sign of bad art, which is soothing people by giving them what they expect.*

DS: The sixties are back!

BR: *Recycling media images and then presenting them as art is very reassuring to people. In the way we were talking about kitsch being evil, that is evil.*

DS: In Herman Broch's lecture notes on the problems of kitsch, he talks about Nero in his garden in Rome. Kitsch culture allows people to see their own spectacle as something quite different from what it is. People are seeing the lie as the truth and the mind doesn't want to accept the lie. They know it's the lie. People are so sincere about the lie, they've got the wink that's saying that it's "irony"—another buzzword for kitsch.

BR: *This presentation of meaninglessness as meaning relieves people and makes them comfortable.*

DS: That's the democratic thing: everybody can be an artist. What makes art? It's what the gallery sells. It's not what the artists say.

BR: *We assign artificial values to certain categories of objects for economic purposes.*

DS: What sells works and what works sells.

BR: *That's a nice way of putting it. In the sixties, people thought things were getting better and better.*

DS: The young people said that; the older people thought that everything was getting worse. The thing that's different is the ways that people are being manipulated. The art world was too small for big-time manipulation. Now it's into big-time manipulation.

BR: *That's because the work of art, because it is an object, has the capacity to fulfill an economic function that is very important, which is to be a medium of exchange. It has been redefined as that.*

DS: I used all kinds of flower pictures for inspirations. Most of the early flower pictures were completely invented by myself. The first big flower painting is the one that is of bright mums in a vase that I took off the urn decorations in the house in St.-Tropez. It was just one that was in the studio. It is actually one of the strangest ones. Then after that, I began to look at other pictures.

BR: *In other words, there was a sculpture of a bouquet of flowers?*

DS: No, the balusters had an urn motif, and I took the architectural device and turned it into a flower pot. Following again the idea of smokestacks and fire, in the lower half of the paintings you always have the pot, the stack, and in the upper levels you always have the gestures or the fire or the flowers.

BR: *Why fire?*

DS: Because it was another industrial flower. You see the smokestacks when they are out as trees, and then you see them with fire blowing and they look like industrial flowers.

BR: *Wonderful poisonous perfume.*

DS: That was the reason that I started using them. I called them blue irises with a gas flame; and I used yellow flame as a yellow iris. Then I moved into the forest fires because I wanted the fires to be more chaotic and yet blocked off and restrained by big volumes and constructions.

   I wasn't interested in portraiture and I wasn't interested in narrative and if I was going to put figures in pictures—which I wanted to use to keep expanding the language—I wanted to place them in a posture that was unavoidable, that all people would have to adopt given the situation. *Figures in the Rain* was one of the first that I worked on, and it had a lot of preliminary sketches because I was trying to use these figures in a way that made sense; I had to mechanize or generalize them somehow, and at the same time keep them human and consistent. I placed the figures in the rain and I drew them with hats and coats so that everything was obscured, all of their human features except for the figures. Then I pelted them with wax, like the rain in perspective; there is a lot of wax rain. I figure that people in the rain and wind have to adopt a defensive posture; given the situation, they will always adopt the same posture. If the wind is blowing, they have to hold their hats down and coats closed with their hands so that everything is held down. Then I worked on the hats to make them almost screws, so that they were almost screwed back into the picture plane. With the firemen, you have the uniform and the men as silhouettes.

BR: *Yes, but is there any meaning to the defensive pose?*

DS: There are certain generic postures that people have to adopt given the situation. That was a defensive one; maybe it is always a defensive one. In the equestrian painting, I had the woman rider adopt a posture in order to stay on the rearing horse. She had to assume a certain posture in order to stay on the horse. Everybody, given that set of circumstances, will either have to do that or get thrown off the horse. The firemen form a barricade between you and the chaos, but at the same time they look helpless, they are all men in uniform, anonymous symbolic figures; they are firemen. That was the way I wanted to approach the figure. I began to see the possibilities in the generic postures and I wanted to expand my paintings into that realm. I didn't want to be involved with portraits; I didn't want to be involved with what the people looked like. But I didn't want figures to be excluded from the work. That was the way I could rationalize using the figure. I don't do it that often, but now and then I have figures in them, and they are basically hanging around.

BR: *What do you mean?*

DS: Most of the time when there are figures in there, they are either fighting or struggling with chaos, like the firemen, or people trying to cope with a missile strike. I did one called *Fairview,* which was a town in New Jersey where a plane smashed into the town and blew it up. Obviously, the carnage at that moment was so intense that all the firemen could do was stand and watch it, at least in the picture that is what I had them do. Just hang around like the furniture.

BR: *What drew you to using the weather or the elements, like fire?*

DS: The first time I started using things like that was when I began to paint the cigarette paintings. No, the first ones were the curved landscapes where I would have an iceberg. Although I wouldn't say that I put the elements in there—the material contained it, by itself.

The landscapes, the matched-tile landscapes with the icebergs in them, islands and sea, were the color of the tile. Actually, those were important paintings, because they opened up a vista of land-scape for me. I could put linoleum tiles that had striations in them together, and you had a real pictorial depth of looking out at the open sea. This was incredible because it freed me to do anything. These absolutely flat, haphazard materials have enormous depth when presented in a vertical way. I could achieve an absolute flatness with deep space. That's what started the whole thing. Then when I started elaborating the imagery more, after doing the icebergs and schematizing it, I began to see that when one thinks of the square of the picture, you might as well use every element available to you. If you are going to put elements together, you might as well use elements that include the things you can't see—air, wind. When I got to the cigarettes, the only way I could differentiate between the hard plaster smoke and the hard tile, except for the edges, was to have the smoke affected by wind or air, to have it blow. That brought in the use of light and air. One of the last of the cigarette paintings summed up the whole gamut of the puzzle pieces in the smoke rings. I had the cigarette drop down and I had formed out of the smoke a perfect ring. That was the crux of everything I was trying to say at the time—all of painting is really like blowing smoke rings. There is such an ephemeral relationship between gesture and structure, like a smoke ring. That led me into using the fires, trying to make something out of energy, contrasting gesture and really rigid structure. Which is what I continue to try to do even in the newest ones, like *Rail Strike,* where I have a struck railroad yard with a lot of detailed drawing and a lot of deep perspective. Once again, there is all this structure that is stopped and stuck and useless until a point is won and it is agreed to make it go again.

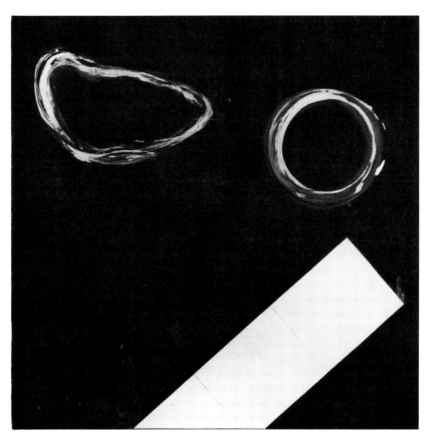

SMOKE RINGS APRIL 14, 1981.
Tar, oil and spackle on tile over wood; 48″ x 48″.
Courtesy Blum Helman Gallery, Inc., New York.
Photo: Roy M. Elkind.

BR: *When did you make your first prints?*

DS: I was making tar drawings, which is what you saw at Willard Gallery in 1978, those big three-sided drawings with tar dropped across them. I had a show at the New Museum; I was in one of the first shows that Marcia Tucker had ever put together after she left the Whitney and was forming a museum and didn't have a gallery or a space and they were putting shows together in different places. This one was in Tokyo in about 1977 and they had a little catalogue. Then she moved to her space at the New Museum and started having shows on Fifth Avenue at the New School and she decided to do a re-exhibition of all those "first shows" that she had done that were never seen in New York. I put in two of the tar drawings and Bob Feldman of Parasol Press came over to me and said, "Do you want to do some prints?" I said okay, and he said that he would send me out to California to work at Crown Point Press and I could do whatever I wanted. They would put me up at a hotel and I could just work. I had not really done much printing except in college. I got there and I thought, "Now what am I going to do?" The logical thing to do was to continue with the little square paintings—small, one-foot-square plates—and make a lot of them and continue the rearranging of objects I had been doing in the puzzle pieces. Go through all of the permutations and then something else would happen—maybe I would invent a few new ones that I could use in the paintings. I treated them like drawings in a way. That's how I got started. I got some images from them that led into the cigarettes, but, at the time, I was doing small ones like *Hat, Cane and Moon, Pie + Dress* and *Baseball Bat and Ball.*

BR: *Is* Hat, Cane and Moon *a reference to Magritte?*

DS: No, these were called puzzle pieces, where I would take a derby hat and brim and then break it apart and you would have a half moon and a cane, or I would take a dress that was sliced in half and put together again and you would have a pie, or a shirt sliced up into a pair of pants and a skirt, a boat turned upside-down into a table. There were a number of these things. I thought that it would be a good way to make a series of prints, so I started doing those. The first one was called *Water Under the Bridge;* it was kind of a pun on the fact that the print thing was over. I had done these prints with boat imagery—sailor hats and this and that—and it was basically finished. It was another permutation of the way I was thinking about the prints. Then Feldman sent me to France. I have been printing ever since.

BR: You explained the aquatint process and how you've used it in an unconventional way in the lemons.

DS: It was like the photographic thing that we were talking about before, where you take a simple Polaroid and suddenly you find yourself on the cutting edge of space-age technology, out there waiting in limbo, seeing possibilities that never existed before, just to do the simplest thing. While I was doing the charcoal drawings of the lemons, the edges were breaking down more and more, getting fuzzier and fuzzier and I was building up the powder of the charcoal, and I started thinking that since I am involved in the industrial and urban aspects of fruit and generic images, why not take it to the next step, which would be mechanical reproduction using industrial materials, like copper and acid. The first one was the small aquatint of a tulip, which was the frontispiece of a little poetry book for a young woman poet, April Bernard. Then I made a series of little tulips, very small, where we would drop the aquatint and take it out of a box, and before it was melted I would remove the particles I didn't want to be black to actually make the drawing in powder. Then I would melt the aquatint. That would give me these very mysterious, dark and smoky and sooty edges and they were just like drawings. I thought that this was suitable. Then I wanted to increase the scale and make giant lemons—I wanted to make them so that they were not like the drawings—so I made them one size larger. Then the problem was how to do a plate that big and move it so that it could be worked on without all of the powder being disturbed. Parasol Press decided to invest in building an entire studio to do it, since I was using the biggest aquatint box ever built. Gerald Parker worked for about a year figuring out how to do it. He finally figured out that the simplest thing to do is not to move the plate, but to move the air.

BR: *How do you mean?*

DS: You put up a big box and you move the box over the plate and you drop the aquatint and when you are through you move the box away and you leave the plate. You really move the air that contains the resin, and the plate doesn't have to move. If you are building a print studio, you might as well start with the biggest, because then it works for everybody's stuff. It will work for little things as well as big things.

BR: *Do you think that spending part of the year in Europe every year affects your work?*

DS: Yes, a lot of the involvement that I had with the lemons really did. I got a lot of source material from the beaches in St.-Tropez. I used a lot of the flowers out of the garden. It's just different; the light is different and all of these things are different and I use it, but I am not sure that it really informs the paintings. A lot of the paintings I start in New York and finish there.

BR: *You have them shipped over?*

DS: Yes, I ship everything over. I start them over here and finish them over there or I start things over there and finish them over here. If I am working on a painting over here, I don't stop; I send it over and finish it. I don't have that much time there and I like to do a lot of work, so I am always two or three steps into different paintings at different times. I need people helping me doing the manual labor and there is always something for them to do. I like to start with them working on one thing while I am doing something else so that when I am through with that, they can move on to what I have just done and I can go back and work on what they have just done; it is a dialogue that keeps the paintings moving along at a speed that I can deal with without waiting and losing momentum.

BR: *Do you work on more than one picture at a time?*

DS: Yes. I try to work on as many different images as I can at one time. I like to work on flowers and fruits and dark pictures all at the same time.

BR: *Don't you think that the greater amount of detail in your work has something to do with living part of the year in Europe, where there is so much more detail? The nuances in the architecture and the different kind of landscape, you don't have endless stretches of land, there is always some kind of incident.*

DS: I'm not sure. I would not say that I am conscious of it, but one of the reasons I work on different things at the same time is that if I am doing a complicated, dark picture, then the flower picture will tend to be very simple and quick, and the fruit picture will be in between. If I am working on a very complicated flower picture, the dark picture will tend to be simpler. I try to work on different aspects of spontaneity in each picture so it keeps satisfying different elements at different times.

BR: *Don't you think that it is odd that you are sitting there on the water in St.-Tropez and you don't paint it?*

DS: I don't think it's odd. I sit in restaurants all the time and I don't paint the people in the restaurants. When I was in Majorca in 1979 I did a lot of those little boat pictures while I was sitting overlooking the water; there wasn't anything else to look at. But St.-Tropez is like a city; it is like being anywhere else. The small still lifes take over there and I do them from the markets, because there is such a variety of fruits and fresh things, things you don't see here, like the almonds with the little fuzzy knobs and all that. I always paint an egg white and I paint a lemon black and I set them all up like that. They don't have white eggs over there.

BR: *You literally paint the egg?*

DS: I spray paint it.

BR: *Because it's not white?*

DS: Because it's not white. Somehow, putting a brown egg in it defeats the purpose.

BR: *What is your ambition as an artist?*

DS: My ambition as an artist is to matter.

BR: *In what sense? In the history of art?*

DS: Yes, to have actually accomplished a picture that makes it impossible for people to look at future painting without looking through me. The great thing about real art is that it always freaks out people's preconceptions. Like the little story that Herman Broch tells, first it takes away your eyesight and then it gives it back to you. First it makes you blind and then it gives you back your sight. I think that's really great: real art makes people blind and then gives them back their sight. They have never been anywhere else. Let me read you the story:

> In a Jewish community in Poland a miracle-working rabbi appeared one day with the gift of restoring sight to the blind. Ailing men and women came from far and wide to Chelowka—that is the name of the community —and among them one Leib Schekel, plodding along the dusty country road, protecting his eyes with a green eye-shield and holding his blind-man's stick. An acquaintance of his came along: "Hey there, Leib

Schekel, you are off to Chelowka!" "Yes, I'm going to see Him at Chelowka." "And what's happened to your eyes?" "My eyes? What's the
matter with my eyes?" "If your eyes are still all right at your age, why on
earth are you going to Chelowka with your stick?" Leib Schekel shakes
his head: "Because a man who is still fit at a hundred can be short-sighted.
Don't you see what I mean? When I am before Him, the Great and True,
I shall be blind and he will give me back my sight."

It is the same with the true work of art. It dazzles you until it blinds
you and then gives you back your sight.

BR: Do you read a lot?

DS: I don't read as much as I should. I am reading *The Guiltless,*
a Herman Broch book. I have read a lot of his writing and I like
it. The last book that I tried to read was *The Bonfire of the
Vanities,* but the only thing that I liked about it was the title. I
don't have that much time to read. I have been reading books
about still life.

*BR: You told me that you were thinking of writing a book about still
life.*

DS: I am in the middle of sorting through it. One of the things
I do when I get curious about a particular picture is I start trying
to think about *why* we paint this thing.

BR: Why do you paint still life?

DS: I paint still life because I thought it was the perfect vehicle
for advancing art. If I was going to be involved in abstraction
and painting and figuration, still life was perfect because it could
be very abstract and I could put a lot of things back into abstract
paintings that had been removed, like space and volume and
light. I could put in meaning and I could use black lemons
and industrial things. I could work with scale and eroticism and
sexuality and all of the kinds of things that you find in life. The

still-life fascination came from the lemon. Initially, the lemon was just emblematic. I began stacking them like in the drawings, using shading to create volume. I began to think, "How does the still life in general function in Western art?" Since about 1598, it has become an important vehicle for advancing art.

BR: *How do you mean?*

DS: If you think of painting from the Greeks through the end of the 1500s, you don't really think of still-life painting as great painting. It was not considered great painting.

BR: *It was not a subject in its own right, it was an accessory.*

DS: After that, you can't imagine advanced painting without it. Especially if you think of Impressionists and Cubists and so on. All of that is tied to still life. It became very important.

BR: *As you know, Hans Hofmann's classes were all based on drawing from the figure and still life. All of the students who went to the Hofmann school had to do still life, but then they were determined in an abstract way, any way they happened to see it.*

DS: Once the figure was removed from painting, the secular aspect of it could be eliminated. One could use the object as a medium in which one could explore mathematics and paint surface, and you could change forever the way people looked at paintings. Look at how important still life is to pop art. Warhol said that he saw himself as a still-life painter.

BR: *He said that his portraits were still lifes.*

DS: That's true. Still life is the heir of portraiture. Whenever you are dealing with portraiture you always have the question of likeness. With still life you're free. Anyway, that is what I am exploring with still life and that's one of the reasons why when

I started using it, it made so much sense to me. It's the logical way to go. Again, that's going to be a vehicle to advance painting.

BR: *Why did you paint that first lemon?*

DS: I try to work with imagery that is on the cutting edge, that is both totally abstract and totally what it is. I thought that the lemon was perfect because it is a big mass, a big, black mass of compressed charcoal that *could* be a lemon. It freed me from the attachment to the lyrical qualities of the tulips. That is why I started drawing the first batch. Then I started thinking, why not start making big paintings of these things, because it is time to do that, to make big, yellow lemons.

BR: *Why did you do the tulips?*

DS: I did the tulips because at the time I was working on the paintings that had the industrial irises and the streetlights. These things were hard-edged, and I wanted to make drawings that were looser, that allowed for a lot more drawing without a hard edge, so I started working on a tulip, which I could do as a bulb and then let it wander; I could let it die. You know how tulips tend to wander once you put them in a pot; I thought that would give me a way of freeing my drawing, and then I could try to work with the edges and soften them, put another element into them so it wasn't so hard-edged. It was the other aspects and the other part of my mind—in addition to stoic and rigid things, there are also soft, rounded things. I don't like to sacrifice one thing for the other thing if I can keep both things.

BR: *What's the most important thing about your work that people don't understand?*

DS: That beauty is not an issue.

BR: *You use extremely ambivalent imagery.*

DS: All imagery is ambivalent. That's not the point. The ambivalence of the imagery is not the issue. The issue is what the reason is for using imagery and how one uses imagery in painting. It is to advance painting, not to advance imagery.

BR: *And it comes out of your sense of abstraction being burned out.*

DS: It comes out of other people I am interested in—Pollock, Mondrian. I am working out those ideas in painting on what we see today, on what we deal with day to day. I couldn't have gone the other way. Had I been born earlier, I would have been leading everyday things into abstraction. I am coming from the other side; I don't have the luxury of abstraction. I am trying to grapple with and understand imagery and abstraction, and I am trying to deal with it in paintings.

BR: *There is an inevitability of the task that is left to you. In* The Shape of Time, *George Kubler talks about how all artists enter upon a scene at a given moment that has to do with when they are born and the situation they encounter at that time. What you are dealing with and what you are saying is that for painting to remain viable, it has to deal with both abstraction and imagery.*

DS: We are living in a profoundly visual world, and a visual world that is rectangles and squares.

BR: *It is a world of reproduced images that come from photographs or film. Everything, the square tube.*

DS: This has never happened before.

BR: *Everything that we perceive visually comes to us as a square or rectangle.*

DS: That is why I think that this is an extraordinarily rich moment.

BR: *What you are doing and what I believe Johns and Rauschenberg did was not deny the fact of mechanical reproduction, but continue to paint nonetheless. They don't fall into the trap of painting supergraphics or images that share the qualities of nonsurface or flatness of reproduction. They are the critical people in the sense that they said, "We are not going to deny anything, we are going to accept it all. We are not going to hide from any of this or the fact that our culture perceives in another way." And that way is conditioned by mechanical reproduction. They didn't make paintings based on reproductions or that were reproductions. Their paintings are very clearly handmade by an individual with a particular sensibility. That is why, in a sense, they are heroic figures. At least they did that. Imagine if they had not accepted that responsibility.*

DS: We are doing it still.

BR: *The point is, they did it. They did not hide out from anything that was going on. Neither of them are conceptual artists. Johns is an artist who works out of his own attempt to understand himself, which has so far resulted in him not coming to any conclusions. Rauschenberg's impulse is messianic; it has to do with the fact that he was raised in this crazy holy-roller atmosphere and wanted to become what is now a TV preacher. He wants to save the world. Between Rauschenberg's messianism and Johns's attempt to understand himself, you have two very confused but very authentic people. These are not people who are working out of false sentiment or bad faith or contrivance or preconception or strategy. They are working out of themselves and their best attempts to come to terms with the world and themselves. As a stance, I find it admirable.*

DS: And Americans love it. Why do people think that Johns is the inventor of pop art?

BR: *He wasn't. The American* Flag *was after Larry Rivers's Washington Crossing the Delaware. But Johns's bronze casts of actual-size objects must have influenced you. Why did you cast the lemon?*

DS: I cast the lead lemon in 1985 or '86. Since I am involved in the idea of objects being abstract and also unnatural, I decided that if I was going to cast a fruit, I wanted to cast it in lead, which would be poisonous. I also wanted to mechanize and further standardize the lemon. In other words, all of the lemons, being generic, going the Sunkist route in which they all look the same, I would take one and reproduce it over and over again, up to eight. I thought of it as the next step from the beer cans.

BR: *That is what I am curious about, because it seems that that is what it is.*

DS: It was to say that in the first cast you took a man-made object and you turned it into a sculpture and in this case you take a natural object and you turn that into a sculpture. It was a reverse dialogue. It was a solidifying something that was soft—but further, that the lemons have been so genetically altered that they are the same thing as a beer can.

BR: *Did you ever make the others?*

DS: Yes, I made all eight of them. They are all the same lemon. It also looks like a hand grenade. In fact, I was afraid to take it across borders in the airports because I kept thinking that they were going to find this thing in my bag and they were going to start scattering.

BR: *It looks lethal.*

DS: It feels that way, too. In only one place did they catch it going through the metal detectors; I think that was in Spain.

BR: *Could you describe the process of making your work?*

DS: They start in two ways. The black ones with the rubber backgrounds, the fruits and the flowers, first come as white tiles on board. They are put on the floor and then I put coats of liquid rubber on them; that's the first step. It's soft and then it hardens, so that makes the black. It comes out of caulking tubes; it's for flashing and road repair. It gets two or three, usually three, coats so there is a drying time of about two weeks while they are on the floor, before they are ready to get up. Then the center parts are trimmed—the early ones weren't trimmed—and the panels are put on the wall one at a time and they are fitted together to make a kind of canvas. The tiles are already stuck down; the structure is already done when I put the black on.

BR: *And there is this irony in that you are using a stretcher on which canvas would normally be stretched. Instead of using canvas for a support, you put Masonite on it.*

DS: Of course, then there are the pipes that go on. The tiles and Masonite float off the stretcher bar on little metal pipes.

BR: *The surface projects and it is explicitly surface and explicitly flat no matter what illusion you are creating, because you see it as something that is projected in front of the stretcher bars.*

DS: I make the drawing directly on the tile with black crayon and I erase it by scraping it off with a razor blade so I get the drawing I want. Then I will paint in the imagery that I want with black house paint right on the tile. All of the "disaster" pictures come the same way as the white ones except that they have blue tile on them and those go directly on the wall without surface preparation. Once they are on the wall, I draw on them like on a blackboard, with oilstick.

BR: *Do you have preliminary drawings?*

DS: No, I usually don't. I usually have a Polaroid of a fruit or flowers in the studio which I will photograph and work with. I always keep flowers in the studio. For these, I take chalk and draw on the tile like a blackboard until I get the image that I want. I can erase it with water and a sponge and redraw it. Once I get the drawing I want on the black rubber, I will go over it with white oilstick so that when I am cutting out those areas, the chalk doesn't burn away, you can always see it.

BR: *What do you mean by cutting out?*

DS: That is the next step, where you use a blowtorch and knives to cut out the areas inside the cartoon. All of the tar, the rubber, everything gets cut out, back down to the Masonite. The cut-away areas are first gessoed and then filled in with spackle.

BR: *It's almost an inlay.*

DS: Yes, it's like rebuilding walls with two different surfaces. Then, once the layers of the spackle have been put on up to the surface and sanded smooth, I paint it with oil paint. I usually put on the oil paint with trowels and then take turpentine and rags and go back over it with my hands and wash it out. I start taking the color back off and soaking the color into the spackle or into the tar.

BR: *Do you think that technique is a means to innovation?*

DS: Sometimes. I'm not sure that it always is. You develop your technique in order to achieve something and sometimes you get into a dialogue between you and the thing you are working on. The technique will say something else that you hadn't thought of and you go back and do it a different way. Sometimes it can be innovative and sometimes not.

BR: *Your working and way of painting and the materials you use are so different from what we think of as painting, that by definition it makes the work look different.*

DS: That goes back to doing all of this in order to escape the illustrative. That is one of the reasons that it evolved. When you paint on canvas, it works the same way; you draw on the canvas, fill it in with black paint, fill in the blacks with a brush tar, and then wash that with turpentine to seep it out to unify the surface. Sepia is a seepage from tar—that is the color sepia; this is rubber. I can add a brown color into the pots of rubber so that it will have a sepia tone, sometimes not so it can be gray and cold. But very little color, just to tip it. Then I take yellow and I put in the sky or the fire or whatever. It's always the same two colors. Then the cartoon is complete.

BR: *You speak of the cartoon; nobody would use that word today, but that is the way the old masters worked, from a full-scale drawing. Even though you don't work from drawing, the fact that the tiles create a visible grid makes the look resemble in some ways old-master cartoons for paintings.*

DS: If you saw one at that stage, it looks like a finished painting, except that that is the drawing, very contrast-y and bright.

BR: *Again, there is a contradiction. You are not using a cartoon, you are not using a sketch or a drawing; you are drawing directly on the surface. There is not any pre-existing drawing on a grid like Gorky's early portraits, where you see that the technique is the way that drawings were always translated into paintings, or the way in which a drawing served as the structure of a painting—the grid was necessary so that you could get exact duplication.*

DS: It is an irony, but the reason that you would do a drawing first for a classical mural or a fresco is that if you drew on the walls, you would have to scrape it down, and by the time you were through filling the wall back in, you would have a bumpy surface. So they had to draw it first and then transfer it to the wall. The way I do it, I can scrape and eliminate and change the drawing. Basically, I do have a cartoon, but there is no paper. Occasionally, when I was doing canvas from the tile in order to gauge the differences of the illusory space, I would literally, onto big sheets of tracing paper, trace the original cartoon on the tile and then literally transfer the big drawing right onto the canvas. So I had two practically identical images to work with in two different ways. I do the lemons the same way; I do a tracing of one lemon and then all the drawings come off of the tracing.

BR: *Are you consciously working with the idea of replication or the relationship of originals to replicates?*

DS: It is a convenience. I do it rather that putz with the same drawing again. I already have the drawing, why not just trace it?

BR: *By doing the same image on two different surfaces, there is a statement about the impossibility of handmade replication because it is just going to be different.*

DS: These things come after the fact. I wanted to see if there would be any way to make them pretty much identical, but there isn't. The spaces, the surfaces, are very different. It opened up two different kinds of space, which is why I keep doing it. But now I don't necessarily make one painting from the other painting, although I am still very attracted to that idea: making two, one this way and one that way, but not having them as diptychs. I am very involved in that idea.

BR: *What does that idea mean to you? Alternate solutions, more than one solution to a problem?*

DS: Yes, and there are so many different ways of thinking about the same image. It is almost like two different images reveal two different truths or two different ways of dealing with it. In a way, it is pushing the imagery, which sometimes gets very complicated, to a more abstract way of thinking about imagery. But they are not mechanically reproduced, so they are totally different—the space is different and everything is different. I even imitate the tile surface with the paint. I had the blues mixed by computer—you take a piece of tile to the paint store and they use those scanners to make that shade of blue. Unfortunately, the computer isn't completely accurate and it made the darker blue, so I had to go out and get one that matched by eye to make the lighter blue, because there are two blues in the tile. Then I made striations of white marks and then blue, so I really make the tile image with paint. It's silly, but it works, because the reason I like that blue is that in addition to giving a flat surface to work on with the blue-gray that takes the paint well, the white marks and flecking through it add a depth to the surface. They set up a dynamic to begin with. I figured that I already liked that, so why mess with it and flatten it out? When you put all that paint on by hand, the washing of the tar cuts into that surface in a very different way: the tiles are nonporous and flat, so the tar sits up on the surface, whereas on the canvas it goes underneath the paint, too, so you get a handwoven or brushy surface. Two totally different ways of looking at space are revealed. There is no way to know without doing it. Also, by doing that, since the washes go underneath the paint on the canvas, the yellows become golden.

BR: *You get a quality of luminosity on the canvas that is not possible otherwise. In doing this experiment, you find that that particular kind of luminosity, which is an illusion, is only producible on canvas.*

DS: Actually, the ones on canvas more resemble the charcoal drawings.

BR: *Modern art begins when the brushstroke is both a brushstroke and a finger or a hand. It is both things simultaneously and explicitly so. It maintains its identity as a brushstroke made out of pigment while at the same time depicting an image. That is why some people consider Goya the first modernist, some people Manet. When did you start painting flowers?*

DS: I think of flowers and flower painting, making drawings of flowers, as metaphors for drawing. You can make an awkward flower, you can make an elegant flower, you can make a beautiful flower, you can make an odd arrangement of flowers, you can make this or that. You're free in your approach to it. It may not be appealing, or it may be awkward, or an awkward color. Flowers exist. And so one makes something and then says, "This is a flower," in terms of drawing.

BR: *It's odd that you should start with the idea of drawing prior to the idea of flowers per se. In fact, the floral still life has been popular since the Renaissance. Painting flowers is a way of saying, "This subject exists and therefore I'm free to interpret it."*

DS: That's what I mean by a metaphor for drawing. When flower drawings were still pretty much decorative motifs, you had Jan Breughel, for example, who was one of the great still-life painters.

BR: *Rubens used him to paint the floral motifs in his paintings. I think they thought of flower paintings as a decorative motif. It doesn't really become autonomous from decoration until the nineteenth century, when Monet and later on Matisse began to say that flower painting was an important subject. Degas begins to paint flowers as people, for example in* The Woman with Chrysanthemums. *One thing I am curious about is your attitude toward still life, which is very different from most contemporary artists. You seem to believe the subject is as important for painting today as in the past.*

DS: I'm not particularly nostalgic for the past. I'm not drawn to it in that sense.

BR: *Artists brought up in the media culture are perfectly happy to say that painting is dead, that the weight of the dead century is too much for us.*

DS: I think that we are modern people and we don't have to worry about being academic. We increasingly rely on visual information. We rely on rectangles and squares; we rely on photography, cinema or television, which comes from those things. Where does the idea that the image is a rectangle come from? Every cinematographer, every photographer looks through the viewfinder to frame his pictures, and uses those images that matter to him. I think that painters control the rectangle; we control the square. We control those things, so increasingly we're more interested in looking at the rectangle. We give people ideas of how to do it. We are free to do that, in ways in which photographers are not. By snapping 1,440 photographs representing one minute of real time, one would think that in the range of all those photographs—you would think that in that range of time—you would be free to control the rectangle, to control the ways in which one finally chooses a photograph as the thing one wants to represent. But the baggage of information in photography is enormous. Most photographers I've known have always been involved with painting, or have wanted to be painters. And why not? Because painters have the freedom to choose an aesthetic. Painters have the freedom to rearrange the rectangle any way they want to. And nobody can really say "boo" about it.

BR: *Yes, but your compositions are clearly related to the framing edge, so how free are you?*

DS: I think pretty free. I disregard the framing edge and have to still fall within it. I deal with the finite edge. No matter where I put it, it's going to be somehow controlled. So I tend to start at the beginning and just let it fall the way it does. The composition looks like it's very much controlled and set up by that edge, but in fact the drawing starts out at a certain point and it ends wherever it ends.

BR: *Do you make preliminary drawings for all of your paintings?*

DS: No.

BR: *How do you start a work?*

DS: Right on the painting.

BR: *How long have you taken photographs?*

DS: I've taken pictures—paintings—from photographs for the past five or six years.

BR: *Are you saying your paintings come from photographs?*

DS: I use photographs for most of them.

BR: *You photograph still lifes, for example, a pear and an apple, which appear in your paintings.*

DS: I used that as a study, as a drawing, basically, for a still life.

BR: *Are you defining photography as drawing?*

DS: No. I use the setups; I set up a still life, photograph it, and work from the photograph. I do the drawing from the photograph on the panel.

BR: *Like Degas?*

DS: Degas used cameras. So did Dürer, in a sense.

BR: *The camera obscura is not a photograph. Photography was not invented until 1849. After 1849, Corot, Renoir and Degas and, as it happens, Bonnard and Gauguin and many other painters used photography. I think the difference between artists who painted exclusively plein-air works in the second half of the nineteenth century and those who used photographs is an important distinction; instead of sitting in a field, they could just record the spontaneous moment of the light passing and take the photograph back to the studio, and many of them did.*

DS: Yes, but prior to that they used the frame and set up a geometric grid and worked from that.

BR: *You're talking about the* camera obscura.

DS: What we're talking about is how people use whatever tools they can in order to prolong the moment so they can work. Canaletto couldn't do the Venice that we see if he had to stand there for four weeks or five weeks or six weeks and do that scene: he set it up and sketched it through grids in order to capture that moment. The *camera obscura* changed the transferral of reality to painting that has been going on for centuries.

BR: *Do you mean that in order to perfect reality you have to freeze it in a photograph?*

DS: No, not simply to attempt to depict reality. All great paintings transform reality and the transformation, before the invention of photography, has to do with doing the preliminary drawings. Delacroix said that you couldn't really consider yourself a draftsman unless you could draw a man falling from a three-story window, before he hit the ground.

BR: *You're thirty-six years old. How many people your age have read Delacroix's journals? Why did you read them?*

DS: Because I'm curious! I think we look at great art of the past and it's all a part of our experience. I want to know why what they did was peculiar. Not that we should do it, or that it's valuable for us to do it, but why is it that they could do what they did? What were their values?

BR: *What is our set of values?*

DS: I think that our set of values is very different. We look at things quicker. We know a lot of information immediately that they didn't know. We are trained in a different way to look at art, so much other information has come to us. We should understand Delacroix, Géricault and why da Vinci would take apart a body to look at the anatomy, or draw it, or why those times demanded a certain thing, and why these times demand other things. That's not to say that we should re-create those things, because I don't think it's important that we do that. They did that very well. We can't do it. As at any other time, our time demands using the information available to us to create original works of art.

BR: *I know you have friends who make movies. Certainly cinema, in many ways, is the art of our time.*

DS: One of the arts of our time. I don't think it is *the* art of our time. In fact, it might have even been better and more of an art of the time thirty years ago. I am a painter and I think that painting is the art of our time. Other things reached a point at which they took over, but now they're bankrupt. Painters never had that problem, we've continued to progress. So now the media has to look at painting, which is one of the reasons cinematographers and film people are involved in painting.

BR: *Kubrick's* Barry Lyndon *was an attempt to animate painting. The greatest directors—Kurosawa, Fellini, Eisenstein—were painters and did their own storyboards. They made their movies to correspond to those visions and that, I think, is extremely interesting.*

DS: It is also important. As I said, painters have always controlled the rectangle. If you look at what we consider great movies, their directors understood that what painting didn't have was motion. But within the motion of the movie, you still have the static frame, and how does one frame those things? In the beginning, as with all great forms of art, the exhilaration of the newness of it, which is the motion, can take over. You have Fred Astaire dancing, you have tracking, you have Orson Welles moving the camera in space. Even in the earliest films, when the train comes into the station, you have a fascination with the one thing that's unique to cinema, and when that wears off, you then have to settle into the business of how to make a movie. Film relies, again, not only on the narrative. Since film and photography can do narrative work better, the best painting has removed itself from narrative work. Narrative painting, I think, is a superfluous idea. The realm of painting is the individual's freedom to act alone. You don't have that, really, except in painting. You don't have that anywhere—in any other medium. You don't have it in photography; you don't have it in cinema. I still think the best photography is a snapshot. I mean, it's the one thing that nothing else can do. A picture of your relatives in front of a monument is what photography can do that nothing else can really do. I take two kinds of photographs, the portraits, which are snapshots in one spot on the porch at St.-Tropez, and the still lifes, which I take because the fruit tends to rot. And I prefer a mechanical flash to daylight.

BR: Why?

DS: Because I think it is closer to the way we tend to see. I think it was Oscar Wilde who said that sex in the twentieth century was all a matter of lighting. You know, I think that's true.

BR: You quote Oscar Wilde a lot. Some of his wittiest epigrams have to do with artificiality.

DS: Well, how do we look at things? I mean, we have control over our lighting in a way that nobody else really had. We are used to seeing things that way. To control by direct light is an artificial way of looking at fruit. But the fruit that we eat is artificial anyhow. So that artificiality follows right straight through.

BR: I heard your MoMA lecture in which you said that finally things begin to resemble each other, then there is a kind of leveling, and *sameness, about experience. I presume it had to do with your experience of the way in which we take in information through reproduction and also the way that everything is altered through chemistry, advertising and the television tube.*

DS: We live in that box, for good or ill, which is why I think you find painters becoming pop stars. People really are used to living in a two-dimensional reality. This is a big problem, but it is also a reality that we do experience things in this way. You're not going to find an apple in the supermarket that looks weird. We now live in a world in which we have a choice between the perfect picture and the real thing. Given the choice, you want what you know, and what you know is a picture of an apple, not so much the apple. That is basically why I go to Europe. In France I go to the markets and I work with the fruits there. Sometimes I'll use natural light, just to see the difference, but in general I like head-on, direct lighting, even though the fruits may be bizarre. The light makes the fruits appear more similar, even if they are different.

BR: Why?

DS: It's a way of looking at things that I think has a lot to do with painting. I think it has a lot to do with the ways in which one can control space, and the ways in which one can control volume. I still think of altering reality in a painting sense. I don't think of trying to re-create another reality so much as I try to think of it as creating a painting space.

BR: You're describing abstraction with its uniform light. If you are essentially an abstract painter, why do you use images?

DS: Because I think that images needed to be put back into abstraction. For me to understand the progression of my own development, and to keep my own interest, I must be able to see a development in how I can move the world. To do that through simply making different colors or adding more surface or putting more stuff in—more sculptural volume on the painting—is a futile exercise. I don't see it leading anywhere. When one can include in the work of art all the things of the outside world—depth, volume—when all of those things can be put into painting and still *be* painting, why deny them? Why not add them in? The march of abstraction through the history of painting leads up to the harmony of pure color or pure geometry, or pure mathematics. Why not take that back into figuration, or figurative works, and alter that perception? It goes both ways. I think of painting in several different ways—one of which is through history, starting with cave painting, as of a mirror existing in the landscape.

BR: *That's so intellectual, and also totally wrong. For all we know about cave paintings, people thought that they were creating magical rituals and they had no perception of abstract representation: they were actually about killing animals for food.*

DS: Well, that may be, but I'm thinking in terms of the way marks were put on the surface. When you paint on a rock, or you paint on a wall, or you paint on a curved surface, or whatever, I think that they disregarded the quality of the surface for the remoteness of it, or the privacy of it. When one paints on a rock, one is not involved with the looking-glass or mirror image that devolved from painting once you go to a flat surface, which starts in Greece with the early murals.

BR: *It starts in Egypt with the fresco.*

DS: Once you start going to a flat surface or a prepared surface, then the surface has an integrity, so you can either look through it or at it. You have either a looking glass or a mirror. In cave painting there is an irregular surface that projects into the room and they put images on it for one reason or another—ritual or whatever—I won't go into all the various complexities of it. I'm just saying, in general, that when you think of flattening that image out and begin to deal with the ways in which you draw on that surface, it opens up to mathematics. It opens up to how to create space on a flat plane, which is where we ended up. Now, imagine taking another leap in the twentieth century, thinking of a rectangle as light—how do you deal with space in a light situation? If you think of film as light, you have a rectangle of light. The reason why I would take a direct photo shot of a still life, instead of allowing the light to fall on the volumes in real space and try to create that, is that I don't see it that way.

BR: *Are you saying that the awareness of reproductive media is a mediating factor for all twentieth-century artists, and inescapable?*

DS: I think so. It is not only a mediating factor, it's baggage that they didn't have, but why can't we use it? They would have used it. Anybody would have used it if he had it. That's the great thing about painting: you use what is available. If you make a painting, knowing what we know, knowing what we know about abstraction, knowing what we know about cave paintings, light and so forth, if you want to put imagery into art in a genuine way, you have to think of all these things. What makes volume and space in a painting is light, or in the case of landscape, Renaissance perspective and geometry.

BR: *There are two types of perspective, linear and atmospheric.*

DS: I have two different kinds of light in a painting. In the still lifes, the flowers, I use a light source to create a volume. If you want to think of how far you can push things, can you make a volume in a painting by using an arbitrary light source? In other words, do you have to have a consistent light source in order to make a realistic painting? Now, if you want to make a painting of an apple *really* a painting of an apple, you have a one-point light source and create volumes. But if you want to make paintings that are relevant in relation to all that we know, why does the light source have to be consistent? You can create forms that appear to be volumes, and have the light come from anywhere. That way, you have both volume and flatness at the same time, since the light source does not follow a rule.

BR: *How do you use light?*

DS: I take a photograph in direct light. Then I change it so that I build up a volume that couldn't possibly happen any other way. It looks as if it could, but it really couldn't.

BR: *Any other way than that?*

DS: If you took a photograph of it and you saw the real thing, it wouldn't look naturalistic. When you look at my paintings, you see all of these volumes, and they lock in together, but they don't follow each light source. They are independent volumes: the black will only be there to support one way of depicting an illusion. It looks realistic, but it really isn't: the light is totally made up. I use light to thwart the photographic sense, but have that perception as a reference. In the landscapes, the dark paintings, I use newspaper photographs as a source because I like a kind of a grayed outline to make those paintings, which I disregard when I make them. I put in all the perspective and all the things that should be in there, and then cover them over with a veneer that gives them almost a processed look. I still maintain the integrity of the drawing, but at the same time disrupt the way in which I depict the image.

BR: *How do you conceive of the relationship of drawing to painting? In your paintings, there's no drawn line. Edge is drawing in your paintings.*

DS: The difference between painting and drawing is volumes and lines. It's almost like a "faux" way of drawing translated into an optical painting. Basically, you fill in what should be a receding line with a flat, plumb line. It's not that I want to thwart perspective, not that I have a set of properties and I want to obliterate them, but I paint over them. It's a way of superimposing one set of principles over another.

BR: *The essence of modernism, and you are an acute instance of it, is self-consciousness. It is assessing situations, criticizing from a dialectical opposition.*

DS: But isn't it the aim of modernism to create a new reality? That is the way I see modernism: as striving to create a new reality that is a true reality.

BR: *True in what sense?*

DS: True in the sense that it is a genuine reflection of the historical perspective. One takes from the past the concepts that led to that painting and builds on them to create a new form of painting or a form of painting that has gathered what we know from them and yet somehow has understood those principles and has gone on beyond that. Not that one thinks of history or life as a linear progression in which there is a winner or some kind of a race toward something. But one does learn and one can add to what we know and come up with a summation of what we know and create a new reality or a new way of looking at all of the things we know about that have come up through that period. Painting is really a complex relationship between the true abilities of man and his ability to deal with the material world. So, in addition to his spiritual life, which changes and grows, or digresses, and changes with the spiritual life of the time, his ability to manipulate the material world is a pretty accurate representation of all of those things put together. If you look at painting purely as the one great mediator between the material world and the world of the intellect, the spiritual life, the ability of man to deal with the material world, it is a slow process. In technological media, or media that remove you from the material world, your ability to manipulate imagery and electronic media puts you out of touch with your ability to deal with the material world. It takes you into a kind of illusory reality that can still deal with the material world but which really is not the material world.

BR: *Why are you so interested in the material qualities of art?*

DS: I think everybody is. No matter what, you have to deal with the material world. I don't mean the material world in the sense of things. The material world in the sense of actual world, reality —you have to deal with that. You don't see it in furniture, you don't see it in crafts, you can't. Those are not the same things.

BR: *Some things you've said could almost be interpreted as a Marxist view of material production.*

DS: My education and my upbringing were involved in a historical and a Marxist view of man's relationship to production. I can't really say how, specifically, I was taught that way; that seems to me to be my education. From high school into college, I decided that I was going to study philosophy. I began to read the early Greeks, up through nineteenth-century German philosophy. I decided that even if I didn't understand it, I was going to read a range of this kind of philosophy.

BR: *Why?*

DS: I don't know. That seemed to be the great intellectual life. A few years ago I realized that Marxism was a nineteenth-century philosophy and that in order to grapple with issues now, or to see the world in a way that would seem to be relevant or true, one had to come up with a different view. I don't have one, per se, but the Marxist theory, or the Marxist way of looking at people in relation to what they produce and their sense of history, can change. History was distorted and is especially distorted now because people don't know what they think. There is so much baggage that one carries, you know, it's like taking a knapsack and going on a journey. I grew up in the mountains, I filled my bag full of canned goods and I realized that it was too damn heavy and I started throwing them away. But then you end up with no food. So in the historical and the "event" pictures, I started taking images that

Veracruz Nov. 18, 1986.
Latex and tar on tile over Masonite; 96½″ x 96½″.
Courtesy Blum Helman Gallery, Inc., New York.
Photo: Bill Jacobson Studio.

were really more about the conflict between chaos and gesture, or between things that one can't see and things that actually really strike you. A lot of the pictures I did weren't disasters, but they were about things that you couldn't see or things that you enter, or of, for instance, a situation where suddenly you couldn't breathe. These things appeal to me because people say that there are no real perpetrators, that things just happen. The people who are producing them are not really aware of exactly what they are producing. They don't really know what these things can do, until there is a situation in which you see the results.

BR: *You're talking about a corporation; you're not talking about individual responsibility. There's only a profit motive.*

DS: Right. These things are totally removed from people's sense of reality, in a way, and that is what drew me. I think it's true of the still lifes, too. I mean, when you look at the fruit that you're eating, it's bizarre, really. When you go to an open market you can pick one thing over another. You go to a normal supermarket and there is no distinction—one is as good as another. People, naturally, fiddle with the stuff, but they're not going to turn up one thing that's better than another. They're all the same.

BR: *Your idea of using fruit as an equalizer is a way of saying that there has been a kind of standardization, a leveling process in what we eat, too.*

DS: One of the first images I painted in the four panel paintings was a steer—the white outline of a steer.

BR: *Why did you do that?*

DS: I did that because everybody was so macho; everybody was involved with these great mythological creatures, like horses or Picasso's bull. I decided to do a steer, which everyone thought was like all these other big metaphorical images. But I had picked a steer from a nineteenth-century Currier and Ives illustration of how to pick breeding steers. Steers are generic animals—castrated animals—they are just produced for food. The other day, in the *Times*, they had three heifers that were all identical—three steers produced by genetic engineering. They've gone even a step further than gelding and hybrids; they now alter the genes to produce a breed, and that could have been a painting. Did you see the picture? It's just another way of looking at life—turning nature and everything else to serve you.

BR: *Let's get back to how you start a painting.*

DS: I know I'm going to make three limes and a tangerine, I know I'm going to use green, I know I'm going to use orange, I know that green and orange are going to do this certain thing, but I don't know that it is going to turn out the way it turns out. And when it turns out the way it's going to turn out, it could either be okay, or it could be terrible. And it turns out to be okay, but that's an accident, in a way, even though I experience that it will turn out okay.

BR: *You don't reject your work?*

DS: I don't reject that much.

BR: *That's really hedging your bets.*

DS: I don't have to reject it, because I can change it. In other words, I don't say something's finished and it's no good, and then I throw it away. I think of it as a field of play, and I work on it until it's okay. I'd gotten three green limes to a certain point, and I took the orange and I knew what I wanted to do, but I put it on there, and it didn't work—it was too red—so I had to figure out a way to make it work, and the only way to make it work was to continuously push on it, change the edge, change the amount of

102

color, change the volume, change the relationship of the orange to the green, without changing the colors, to make it work. You have a certain set of principles governing the difference between a pot and flowers and between a smokestack and a fire—one is architectural, one is natural—and you set that relationship up over and over again. Flowers aren't the same as fire coming out of a smokestack, what you have is kind of ephemeral: the wildness in the growth of flowers, and then the control—which can also be very wild, although it is controlled—in the man-made pottery. But in paintings the pot and flowers may be different, or they may be very similar, more so than in reality.

BR: *Then you're creating a kind of equivalency that Warhol created. You talk about your "disaster" pictures and, of course, that's what Warhol painted. He painted his flowers, and in that sense, you follow Warhol.*

DS: The difference between Warhol's work and mine is that Warhol's were reproductions of human tragedies; they were mechanical, like everything else. My images might be from newspapers, but they're not mechanical. Very seldom are people involved. They are mainly about a level of chaos and the systems to deal with that chaos.

BR: *If you talk about flower paintings and about disaster paintings, you have to say, "Oh, who did that?" Well, Warhol did flower paintings and he did disaster paintings.*

DS: Turner did disaster paintings and Breughel did flower paintings.

BR: *I'm saying, on the contrary, that the consciousness of genre in a depersonalized sense is an essential part of your work. The idea of continuing with conventional genres—history painting, flower painting —I think Andy Warhol did consciously. In taking historical genres as givens, there is a necessity to make them in some way contemporary.*

DS: I am not so much involved in genre in the sense that Andy was involved in the "image." I'm more involved in the actual physical relationship between the image and the eye. One works against theater, and one works against decoration, but all of those things are properties of painting. Personally, I think that narration is the enemy of painting. Still, all painting contains some. Look at the Sistine Chapel for narration.

BR: *It's true there is a certain theatricality about your work, but there's no narration.*

DS: I'm antinarration.

BR: *It is not something that takes place in time, it takes place in space.*

DS: Actually, it does. That's why when somebody says to me, "That painting is so much of its time," I think, "That means they're saying it is not a very good painting," although all paintings are a part of time.

BR: *You sound like a conceptual artist.*

DS: How? That seems very plodding. Conceptual art is a product of the democratization of education. They began to think that all you had to do was think about it and that was enough. It isn't just looking at the image, it is also about having to confront it.

Maybe at first I thought all images were equal. When I did my "debris" paintings, I felt that all imagery—drawings, images, illustrations—all things that could be used in painting had already been used, so it was just a matter of throwing them in there.

BR: *Why did you change your mind?*

DS: I changed only in that one thing led to another. I could do that for a long time and never see any development in my own work. I could continue to throw images in there and it would end up like Arman. Or I could begin to hone down to the point of making a series of random images in which each image could be developed into something quite interesting. One could develop totally separate from the other. If you had a room filled with separate images, you might get the idea that all images were equal, but it turned out that all the images, when confronted, when one had to deal with them, were complex structures in themselves. So I began to pursue all the different complex structures. That's where I ended up, that's what I am doing now.

BR: *Why be a painter today?*

DS: The most ironic thing to do today is to actually be a painter. To be a serious painter now, that's ironic enough.

SOLO EXHIBITIONS

1976 N.A.M.E. Gallery, Chicago.

1977 Artists Space, New York.
      Institute for Art and Urban Resources, P.S. 1 Special
        Projects Rooms, Long Island City, New York: "Turning
        the Room Sideways"

1979 Willard Gallery, New York: "Donald Sultan"
      Young Hoffman Gallery, Chicago: "Donald Sultan"

1980 Willard Gallery, New York: "Donald Sultan"

1981 Daniel Weinberg Gallery, San Francisco: "Donald Sultan:
        Recent Paintings"

1982 Blum Helman Gallery, New York: "Donald Sultan"
      Hans Strelow Gallery, Düsseldorf: "Donald Sultan: Bilder
        and Zeichnungen"

1983 Akira Ikeda Gallery, Tokyo: "Donald Sultan"

1984 Blum Helman Gallery, New York: "Donald Sultan: New
        Paintings"

1985 Blum Helman Gallery, New York: "Donald Sultan: New
        Paintings"
      Barbara Krakow Gallery, Boston: "Donald Sultan Prints
        1979–1985"; traveled to Georgia State University,
        Atlanta; Baxter Gallery, Portland School of Art,
        Maine; Wesleyan University, Middletown,

Connecticut; Asheville Art Museum, North Carolina; California State University, Long Beach.

Gian Enzo Sperone Gallery, Rome: "Donald Sultan"

1986   Blum Helman Gallery, New York: "Donald Sultan: Paintings"

Blum Helman Gallery, New York: "Donald Sultan: Drawings"

A. P. Giannini Gallery, Bank of America, World Headquarters, San Francisco: "Donald Sultan: A Survey"

Galerie Montenay-Delsol, Paris: "Donald Sultan"

Galerie de L'Estampe Contemporaine, Bibliothèque Nationale, Rostonde Colbert, Paris: "Donald Sultan: gravures monumentales"

Greenberg Gallery, St. Louis: "Donald Sultan: Drawings and Paintings"

University Art Gallery, California State University, Long Beach: "Centric 24: Donald Sultan Prints 1979–1985"

1987   Akira Ikeda Gallery, Nagoya, Japan: "Donald Sultan: Paintings"

Blum Helman Gallery, Los Angeles: "Donald Sultan: Recent Paintings"

Museum of Contemporary Art, Chicago: "Donald Sultan"; traveled to Los Angeles Museum of Contemporary Art; Fort Worth Art Museum; Brooklyn Museum.

Blum Helman Gallery, New York: "Donald Sultan: Recent Paintings"

Gian Enzo Sperone Gallery, Rome: "Donald Sultan"

1988   Museum of Modern Art, New York: "Donald Sultan Black Lemons"

Martina Hamilton Gallery, New York: "Donald Sultan Prints & Drawings"

GROUP EXHIBITIONS

1972   Ackland Art Museum, Chapel Hill, North Carolina:
          "36th Annual Student Exhibition."
        Mint Museum of Art, Charlotte, North Carolina:
          "Piedmont Paintings and Sculpture Exhibition."

1973   Ackland Art Museum, Chapel Hill, North Carolina:
          "37th Annual Student Exhibition."
        Gallery of Contemporary Art, Winston-Salem, North
          Carolina.

1974   Wabash Transit Gallery, Chicago.

1975   N.A.M.E. Gallery, Chicago: "George Liebert, Donald
          Sultan."
        Art Institute of Chicago: "Graduate Painters."
        Highland Park Art Center, Highland Park, Illinois:
          "Artists Invite Artists."

1976   Fine Arts Building, New York.
        School of the Kansas City Art Institute, Kansas City,
          Missouri.

1977   Institute of Contemporary Art, Tokyo: "Four Artists'
          Drawings" (exhibition organized by The New Museum
          of Contemporary Art, New York).
        A.C.T. Gallery, Toronto.
        Nancy Lurie Gallery, Chicago.

1978   University Art Museum, Santa Barbara, California:
          "Contemporary Drawing/New York."

The New Museum of Contemporary Art, New York: "Doubletake."

Mary Boone Gallery, New York: "Group Show."

Willard Gallery, New York: "Group Show."

1979　Whitney Museum of American Art, New York: "1979 Biennial Exhibition."

Renaissance Society at the University of Chicago: "Visionary Images."

Daniel Weinberg Gallery, San Francisco: "Bryan Hunt/Donald Sultan."

Texas Gallery, Houston: "A to Z."

Holly Solomon Gallery, New York: "Inside/Outside."

Young Hoffman Gallery, Chicago: "Gallery Artists."

Albright-Knox Art Gallery, Buffalo: "Works on Paper: Recent Acquisitions."

Willard Gallery, New York: "Group Show."

1980　R. H. Oosterom, Inc., New York: "Black, White, Other."

Bard College, Annandale-on-Hudson, New York: "Images."

Young Hoffman Gallery, Chicago: "Lois Lane, John Obuck, Susan Rothenberg, Donald Sultan, John Torreano."

Yarlow/Salzman Gallery, Toronto: "New Work/New York."

Indianapolis Museum of Art: "Painting and Sculpture Today: 1980."

Center for Music, Drama and Art, Lake Placid, New York: "The Olympic Thirteen."

Thomas Segal Gallery, Boston: "Paintings, Sculpture, Drawings, Prints and Photographs."

Bell Gallery, List Art Center, Brown University, Providence, Rhode Island: "Invitational."

Willard Gallery, New York: "Group Show."

1981   University Art Museum, Santa Barbara, California:
            "Contemporary Drawings: In Search of an Image."
        Sidney Janis Gallery, New York: "New Directions: A
            Corporate Collection"; traveled to Museum of Art, Fort
            Lauderdale; Oklahoma Museum of Art, Oklahoma
            City; Santa Barbara Museum of Art; Grand Rapids Art
            Museum (Michigan); Madison Art Center
            (Wisconsin); Montgomery Museum of Fine Arts
            (Alabama).
        Contemporary Arts Museum, Houston: "The Americans:
            The Landscape."
        Artists Space, New York: "35 Artists Return to Artists
            Space: A Benefit Exhibition."
        The Museum of Modern Art, New York: "Black &
            White."
        The High Museum of Art, Atlanta: "New Acquisitions."
        Dallas Museum of Fine Arts: "New Acquisitions."
        Art Institute of Chicago: "New Acquisitions."
        Willard Gallery, New York: "Group Show."
        Zabriskie Gallery, New York: "Lois Lane, John Obuck,
            Susan Rothenberg, Donald Sultan, John Torreano."
        Whitney Museum of American Art, New York: "Prints:
            Acquisitions 1977–1981."
        Addison Gallery of American Art, Andover,
            Massachusetts: "New, Now, New York."
        Blum Helman Gallery, New York: "Bryan Hunt, Neil
            Jenney, Robert Moskowitz, Donald Sultan."
1982   Indianapolis Museum of Art: "Painting and Sculpture
            Today: 1982."
        Blum Helman Gallery, New York: "Drawings."
        Margo Leavin Gallery, Los Angeles: "Selected Prints:
            Jennifer Bartlett, Jim Dine, Jasper Johns, Elizabeth
            Murray, Donald Sultan, Robert Rauschenberg."
        Brainerd Art Gallery, State University of New York at

Potsdam: "20th Anniversary Exhibition of the Vogel Collection"; traveled to Gallery of Art, University of Northern Iowa, Cedar Rapids.

1983   Daniel Weinberg Gallery, Los Angeles: "Drawing Conclusions: A Survey of American Drawings: 1958–1983"; traveled to Daniel Weinberg Gallery, San Francisco.

Museum of Modern Art, New York: "Prints from Blocks —Gauguin to Now."

San Francisco Museum of Modern Art: "Selections from the Permanent Collection: Graphics."

John Berggruen Gallery, San Francisco: "Selected Works."

Margo Leavin Gallery, Los Angeles: "Black & White."

Castelli Graphics West, New York: "Black & White: A Print Survey."

Barbara Krakow Gallery, Boston: "Rare Contemporary Prints."

Daniel Weinberg Gallery, Los Angeles: "Seasons Greetings."

Palacio de Velásquez, Madrid: "Tendencias en Nueva York": traveled to Fundación Juan Miró, Barcelona; Musée du Luxembourg, Paris.

The Brooklyn Museum, New York: "The American Artist as Printmaker."

Blum Helman Gallery, New York: "Steve Keister: Sculpture/Donald Sultan Charcoals."

1984   Museum of Fine Arts, Boston: "Brave New Works: Recent American Painting and Drawing."

Whitney Museum of American Art, Downtown Branch, New York: "Metamanhattan."

Getler/Pall/Saper, New York: "Prints, Drawings."

Museum of Modern Art, New York: "An International Survey of Recent Painting and Sculpture."

Jeffrey Hoffeld & Company, Inc., New York: "Little
Paintings."
Blum Helman Gallery, New York: "Drawings."
Fuller Goldeen Gallery, San Francisco: "50 Artists/50
States."
Musée d'Art Contemporain, Montreal: "Via New York."
Margo Leavin Gallery, Los Angeles: "Eccentric Image(s)."
New Math Gallery, New York: "Rediscovered
Romanticism in New York City."
Art and Architecture Gallery, University of Tennessee,
Chattanooga: "Images on Paper Invitational."
Walker Art Center, Minneapolis: "Images and
Impressions: Painters Who Print"; traveled to Institute
of Contemporary Art, University of Pennsylvania,
Philadelphia.
Kitakyushu Municipal Museum of Art, Tobataku,
Kitakyushu, Japan: "Painting Now."
Summit Art Center, Summit, New Jersey:
"Contemporary Cuts."
Artists Space, New York: "A Decade of New Art."
Harcus Gallery, Boston: "The Painter, the Poet, the
Printer, the Playwright, the Publisher, and the Product
. . . a selection of small press edition books made by
artists."

1985   Hill Gallery, Birmingham, Michigan: "Image & Mystery."
Des Moines Art Center: "Iowa Collects."
Thomas Segal Gallery, Boston: "Still Life."
Aspen Art Center, Colorado: "American Paintings 1975–
85: Selections from the Collection of Aron & Phyllis
Katz."
Holly Solomon Gallery, New York: "Innovative Still
Life."
Daniel Weinberg Gallery, Los Angeles: "Now and Then:
A Selection of Recent and Earlier Paintings, Part II."

Joe Fawbush Editions, New York: "Works on Paper."
Martina Hamilton Gallery, New York: "Works on Paper."
Larry Gagosian Gallery, Los Angeles: "Actual Size: An
  Exhibition of Small Paintings and Sculpture."
Janie C. Lee Gallery, Houston: "Charcoal Drawings
  1880–1985."
Laforet/Museum Harajuku, Tokyo: " 'Correspondences':
  New York Art Now"; traveled to Tochigi Prefectural
  Museum of Fine Arts, Utsunomiya, Japan.

1986 Galerie Adrien Maeght, Paris: "A Propos de Dessin."
Jack Tilton Gallery, New York: "The Inspiration Comes
  from Nature."
Janie C. Lee Gallery, Houston: "Paintings, Sculpture,
  Collages and Drawings."
Willard Gallery, New York: "50th Anniversary
  Exhibition."
The Brooklyn Museum, New York: "Public and Private
  American Prints Today"; traveled to Flint Institute of
  Art, Flint, Michigan; Rhode Island School of Design,
  Providence; Museum of Art, Carnegie Institute,
  Pittsburgh; Walker Art Center, Minneapolis.
Greg Kucera Gallery, Seattle: "Recent Prints/Works on
  Paper."
Michael Kohn Gallery, Los Angeles: "Still Life/Life Still."
John Berggruen Gallery, San Francisco: "Selected
  Acquisitions."
Patrick & Beatrice Haggerty Museum of Art, Marquette
  University, Milwaukee: "Romanticism and Cynicism in
  Contemporary Art."
Fuller Goldeen Gallery, San Francisco: "50 Artists/50
  States."
The Brooklyn Museum, New York: "Monumental
  Drawings: Work by 22 Contemporary Americans."
Martina Hamilton Gallery, New York: "Brand-New Prints
  III."

McIntosh/Drysdale Gallery, Washington, D.C.: "David Schwarz: Architectural Drawings/Donald Sultan: New Works on Paper."

Barbara Krakow Gallery, Boston: "Drawings."

Gallery Casas Toledo Oosterom, New York: "Drawings."

Galeria Carnini, Florence: "Biachi·Dessi·Gallo·Schnabel·Sultan."

Akira Ikeda Gallery, Nagoya, Japan: "Drawings."

Museum of Contemporary Art, Los Angeles: "Individuals: A Selected History of Contemporary Art, 1945–1986."

Museum of Fine Arts, Boston: "Boston Collects: Contemporary Painting and Sculpture."

1987 Willard Gallery, New York: "Prints: Rothenberg, Lane, Goldberg, Sultan and Hunt."

Visual Arts Museum, New York: "Still Life: Beyond Tradition."

Art Gallery of Ontario, Toronto: "Selections from the Roger and Myra Davidson Collection."

University Art Gallery, Sonoma State University, Rohnert Park, California: "The Monumental Image."

Whitney Museum of American Art, Stamford, Connecticut: "The New Romantic Landscape."

James Goodman Gallery, New York: "Black and White."

Plaza Gallery, San Francisco: "Big Stuff."

Martina Hamilton Gallery, New York: "Brand-New Prints IV."

Paris–New York–Kent Fine Art, Kent, Connecticut: "22 Artists—The Friends of Louise Tulliver Deutschman."

Richard Green Gallery, Los Angeles: "Contemporary Masters."

1988 Art Gallery/California State University, Northridge: "The Monumental Image."

COLLECTIONS

Ackland Art Museum, University of North Carolina, Chapel Hill.
Addison Gallery of American Art, Andover, Massachusetts.
Albright-Knox Art Gallery, Buffalo.
Arkansas Art Center, Little Rock.
Art Institute of Chicago.
Australian National Gallery, Canberra.
BankAmerica Corporation.
Dallas Museum of Fine Arts.
Des Moines Art Center.
Fogg Art Museum, Harvard University.
Fort Worth Art Museum.
High Museum of Art, Atlanta.
Hirshhorn Museum and Sculpture Garden, Washington, D.C.
Kitakyushu Municipal Museum of Art, Tobataku Kitakyushu, Japan.
La Jolla Museum of Contemporary Art.
Metropolitan Museum of Art, New York.
Museum of Fine Arts, Boston.
Museum of Modern Art, New York.
Neuberger Museum, State University of New York at Purchase.
St. Louis Art Museum.
San Francisco Museum of Modern Art.
Solomon R. Guggenheim Museum, New York.
Toledo Museum of Art.
Walker Art Center, Minneapolis.

BIBLIOGRAPHY

"Reviews: Donald Sultan at N.A.M.E." *Chicago New Art Examiner,* March 1975.

Artner, Alan. "Initially Speaking, N.A.M.E. Spells Creative Cooperation." *Chicago Tribune,* January 25, 1976.

Zimmer, William. "Like the Floor of Old Kitchens." *The Soho Weekly News,* February 10, 1977, p. 16.

"Name Book I: Statements on Art." *The Soho Weekly News,* October 6, 1977, p. 29.

Zimmer, William. "Don Sultan: Room 207, P.S. 1." *The Soho Weekly News,* November 24, 1977, p. 48.

Tucker, Marcia. *Four Artists: Drawings* (exhibition catalogue). Interview by Michiko Miyamoto. New York: The New Museum, 1977.

Rush, David. "Contemporary Drawing—New York." *Artweek,* March 11, 1978.

Frueh, Joanna. "Book Review." *Art in America,* May–June 1978, p. 25.

Frank, Peter. "Art." *The Village Voice,* July 3, 1978, p. 84.

Tatransky, Valentin. "Group Show: Mary Boone." *Arts Magazine,* September 1978, p. 29.

Ratcliff, Carter. "New York Letter." *Art International,* October 1978, p. 55.

Sloane, Harry Herbert. "For Art's Sake: Five of New York's Creative Forces." *Gentlemen's Quarterly,* November 1978, pp. 138–9.

Morgan, Stuart. "Ebb Tide: New York Chronicle." *Artscribe,* 14, pp. 48–9.

Rush, David. *"Contemporary Drawing—New York"* (exhibition catalogue). Santa Barbara: University Art Museum, 1978.

Zimmer, William. "Drawn and Quartered." *The Soho Weekly News,* January 18, 1979.

———. "Building Materials." *The Soho Weekly News,* March 8, 1979, p. 53.

Schwartz, Ellen. "Donald Sultan: Willard." *Art News,* May 1979, p. 170.

Reed, Dupuy Warwick. "Donald Sultan: Metaphor for Memory." *Arts Magazine,* June 1979, pp. 148–9.

Frank, Peter. "Rates of Exchange." *The Village Voice,* June 18, 1979.

McDonald, Robert. "The World Simply Seen." *Artweek,* August 25, 1979.

Lauterbach, Ann. "Donald Sultan at Willard." *Art in America,* September 1979, p. 136.

Zimmer, William. "Art Goes to Rock World on Fire—The Pounding of a New Wave." *The Soho Weekly News,* September 27, 1979, p. 33.

Larson, Kay. "A Group Show: Willard Gallery." *The Village Voice,* October 1, 1979.

"Asheville Artist Holds Show in New York." *Asheville Citizen,* October 28, 1979.

Frank, Peter. "Where Is New York." *Art News,* November 1979, pp. 58–62.

1979 Biennial Exhibition (exhibition catalogue). New York: Whitney Museum of American Art, 1979.

Ratcliff, Carter. *Visionary Images* (exhibition catalogue). Chicago: Renaissance Society at the University of Chicago, 1979.

Raynor, Vivien. "Corporation Builds a Collection that Stresses Youth." *The New York Times,* February 3, 1980, sec. 23, p. 17.

Russell, John. "Art: The Zeitgeist Signals Just Downstairs on 73rd Street." *The New York Times,* February 3, 1980, p. 25.

Larson, Kay. "Small Talk." *The Village Voice,* February 11, 1980, p. 71.

Nye, Mason. "Donald Sultan." *The New Art Examiner,* March 1980.

Phillips, Deborah C. "Donald Sultan: Willard." *Art News,* March 1980, p. 117.

Tolnick, Judith. "Invitational." *Art—New England,* March 1980, p. 11.

Whelan, Richard. "New Editions: Donald Sultan." *Art News,* March 1980, p. 117.

Christiansen, Richard. "Morton Neumann: How the Hell Did I Collect It All?" *Art News,* May 1980, pp. 90–3.

Mays, John Bentley. "New Work/New York: Intriguing, Annoying Show." *Toronto Star,* July 10, 1980.

Zimmer, William. "Artbreakers: Donald Sultan." *The Soho Weekly News,* September 17, 1980.

———. "Keep Up the Image." *The Soho Weekly News,* September 27, 1980.

Larson, Kay. "Donald Sultan at Willard." *The Village Voice,* October 15, 1980.

Isaacs, Florence. "New Artists of the 80's." *Prime Time,* December 1980, pp. 42–9.

Parks, Addison. "Donald Sultan." *Arts Magazine,* December 1980, p. 189.

Tompkins, Calvin. "The Art World: Boom." *The New Yorker,* December 22, 1980, pp. 78–80.

Lawson, Tom. "The Olympic Thirteen: A Critical Appraisal." *Art at the Olympics,* 1980.

Yassen, Robert. *Paintings and Sculpture Today: 1980* (exhibition catalogue). Indianapolis: Indianapolis Museum of Art, 1980.

Levin, Kim. "Donald Sultan and Lois Lane." *Flash Art,* January–February 1981, p. 49.

Tennant, Donna. "Texas Gallery Artists Attack Same Problems but Use Different Approaches." *Houston Chronicle,* January 10, 1981.

Zimmer, William. "Hunter Captured by the Game." *The Soho Weekly News,* March 4, 1981, p. 50.

Schulze, Franz. "Ree Morton's Art Winks with a Straight Face." *Chicago Sunday Times,* April 5, 1981, pp. 24–5.

Crossley, Mimi. "Review: The Americans: The Landscape." *Houston Post,* April 12, 1981, p. 10AA.

Tennant, Donna. "CAM Exhibit Samples Contemporary Landscapes." *Houston Chronicle,* April 16, 1981, sec. 3, p. 8.

Kalil, Susie. "The American Landscape—Contemporary Interpretations." *Artweek,* April 25, 1981.

Tennant, Donna. "The Americans: The Landscape." *Houston Chronicle,* April 26, 1981.

Zimmer, William. "Private Properties." *The Soho Weekly News,* June 17, 1981, p. 52.

Reed, Susan K. "Mort Neumann's Prophetic Eye." *Saturday Review,* September 1981, p. 29.

Kur. "Galerien: Strelow, Düsseldorf." *Rheinische Post,* November 11, 1981, p. 22.

Cathcart, Linda. *The Americans: The Landscape* (exhibition catalogue). Houston: Contemporary Arts Museum, 1981.

Hunter, Sam. *New Directions: Contemporary American Art* (exhibition catalogue). Princeton: The Commodities Corporation of America, 1981.

Plous, Phyllis. *Contemporary Drawings: In Search of an Image* (exhibition catalogue). Santa Barbara: University Art Museum, 1981.

Recent Acquisitions: Works on Paper (exhibition catalogue). Atlanta: High Art Museum, 1981.

Zimmer, William. *35 Artists Return to Artists Space: A Benefit Exhibition* (exhibition catalogue). New York: Artists Space, 1981.

Russell, John. "Donald Sultan." *The New York Times,* April 30, 1982, p. C24.

Larson, Kay. "Urban Renewal." *New York,* May 3, 1982, p. 70.

[Guisola, Felix]. "Entrevista con Bryan Hunt y Donald Sultan." *Vardar,* June 1982, pp. 4–8.

Ratcliff, Carter. "Contemporary American Art." *Flash Art,* Summer 1982, pp. 32–5.

Henry, Gerrit. "New York Review." *Art News,* September 1982, p. 172.

Larson, Kay. "L'art." *Paris Vogue,* October 1982, p. 347.

Friedrichs, Yvonne. "Klare Profile." *Düsseldorfer Stadtpost,* November 1982.

Coopersmith, Georgia. *20th Anniversary Exhibition of the Vogel Collection* (exhibition catalogue). Introduced by Dorothy Vogel. Potsdam, New York: Brainerd Art Gallery, 1982.

Ferrulli, Helen, and Yassen, Robert A. *Painting and Sculpture Today: 1982* (exhibition catalogue). Indianapolis, Indiana: Indianapolis Museum of Art, 1982.

Madoff, Steven Henry. "Donald Sultan at Blum Helman." *Art in America,* January 1983, p. 126.

Ratcliff, Carter. "The Short Life of the Sincere Stroke." *Art in America,* January 1983, pp. 73–9.

Muchnic, Suzanne. "Survey of American Drawing 1958–1983." *Los Angeles Times,* February 4, 1983.

Becker, Robert. "Donald Sultan with David Mamet." *Interview,* March 1983, pp. 56–8.

Schwartz, Ellen. "What's New in Nueva York?" *Art News,* April 1983, pp. 146–9.

Curtis, Kathy. "Drawn Statements." *Artweek,* April 2, 1983, p. 3.

Brody, Jacqueline. "Recent Prints." *The Print Collector's Newsletter,* May–June 1983, pp. 63–6.

Muchnic, Suzanne. "The Galleries: La Cienega Area." *Los Angeles,* July 8, 1983, part IV, pp. 2–3.

"Recent Prints." *Print News,* September–October 1983, p. 19.

Collado, Gloria. "La experiencia neoyorkina." *Arte Suplemento,* October 1983, pp. 106–7.

Logrono, Miguel. "Tendencias en N.Y.: Art U.S.A. 1983 en Madrid." *Diario,* October 9, 1983, p. 16.

Huici, Fernando. "Las nuevas tendencias de Nueva York se exponen en el Retiro madrileño." *El País* (Madrid), October 11, 1983, p. 31.

Soler, Jaime. "New York, New York." *Diario,* October 12, 1983, p. 19.

Serraller, F. Calvo. "Los bellos ecos del último grito artístico." *El País,* October 15, 1983, pp. 1–2.

Friedrichs, Yvonne. "Donald Sultan in der Galerie Strelow: Klare Profile." *Düsseldorfer Stadtpost,* November 1983.

Ortega, Miguel. "Nada Nuevo." *Guadalimar,* November 1983, pp. 13–18.

García, Angel González. "Vanguardia biológica." *El País Semanal,* November 6, 1983, pp. 141–5.

Willard, Marta. "El sueño american." *Actual,* November 7, 1983, pp. 80–2.

Logrono, Miguel. "Tendencias en Nueva York." *Diario,* November 12, 1983, p. 16.

S.M. "Las tendencias artísticas de Nueva York irrumpen en Madrid." *A.B.C.,* December 1983, p. 9.

Glueck, Grace. "Steve Keister and Donald Sultan." *The New York Times,* December 23, 1983, p. C22.

Giménez, Carmen. *Tendencias en Nueva York* (exhibition catalogue). Madrid: Ministerio de Cultura, 1983.

Kuwayama, Maki. *Donald Sultan* (exhibition catalogue). Tokyo: Akira Ikeda Gallery, 1983.

Walker, Barry. *The American Artist as Printmaker* (exhibition catalogue). Brooklyn, New York: The Brooklyn Museum, 1983, p. 124.

Brenson, Michael. "Review." *The New York Times,* February 17, 1984, sec. 3, p. 24.

Larson, Kay. "Donald Sultan." *New York,* February 27, 1984, p. 59.

Harris, Susan A. "The Concrete and the Ephemeral: Recent Paintings by Donald Sultan." *Arts Magazine,* March 1984, pp. 108–9.

Huici, Fernando. "El día en que Nueva York invado Madrid." *El País,* March 1984.

"Donald Sultan, Black Tulips." *The Print Collector's Newsletter,* March–April 1984.

Warren, Ron. "Donald Sultan." *Arts Magazine,* April 1984, p. 39.

Kuspit, Donald. "Donald Sultan at Blum Helman." *Art in America,* May 1984, p. 178.

Robinson, John. "Donald Sultan." *Arts Magazine,* May 1984, p. 48.

Daigneault, Gilles. "Via New York: La peinture des années 80 en transit à la Cité du Havre." *Le Devoir,* May 5, 1984, p. 25.

———. "Via New York: Opération réussie." *Le Devoir,* May 12, 1984, p. 32.

Baele, Nancy. "N.Y. Artists Dazzle with Size." *The Citizen* (Ottawa), May 19, 1984, p. 33.

Bergeron, Ginette. "Deux marchands de tableaux de New York." *Le Devoir,* May 19, 1984, p. 45.

Le Page, Jocelyne. "New York comme si vous y etiez." *La Presse,* May 19, 1984, p. D22.

Bissonnette, Else. "Via New York, un sourire." *Le Devoir,* May 28, 1984, p. 6.

Russell, John. "American Art Gains New Energies." *The New York Times,* August 19, 1984, sec. 2, p. 1.

Heartney, Eleanor. "Belief in the Possibility of Authenticity." *New Art,* December 1984, pp. 118–21.

Batchen, Geoffrey, et al. *Metamanhattan* (exhibition brochure). New York: Whitney Museum of American Art, Downtown Branch, 1984.

Freeman, Phyllis, ed., et al. *New Art.* New York: Harry N. Abrams, Inc., 1984.

Kurka, Don. *Images on Paper Invitational* (exhibition catalogue). Knoxville: Art and Architecture Gallery, University of Tennessee, 1984.

Kuroiwa, Kyosuke, ed. *Painting Now* (exhibition catalogue). Kitakyushi: Kitakyushi Municipal Museum of Art, 1984.

Lemire, Suzanne, and Meilleur, Martine. "Via New York" (exhibition brochure). Montreal: Musée d'Art Contemporain, 1984.

Pradel, Jean-Louis, ed. *Art 83/84—World Art Trends.* Paris: Jacques Legrand International Publishing, 1984.

Cameron, Dan. "Report from Spain." *Art in America,* February 1985, p. 34.

Cohen, R. H. "New Editions." *Art News,* March 1985, p. 65.

Raynor, Vivien. "Art: Sultan's Tar-on-Tile Technique." *The New York Times,* April 12, 1985, p. C9.

Tomkins, Calvin. "Clear Painting." *The New Yorker,* June 3, 1985, p. 106.

Hughes, Robert. "Careerism and Hype amidst the Image Haze." *Time,* June 17, 1985, pp. 78–83.

"Donald Sultan Prints." *The Print Collector's Newsletter,* September–October 1985, p. 137.

Bonetti, David. "Galleries: Jackson Pollock, Expatriates, and Resident Stars." *The Boston Phoenix,* October 1, 1985, sec. 4.

Temin, Christine. "Chic Prints by Sultan; Steel Sculpture by Caro." *The Boston Globe,* October 23, 1985.

Brenson, Michael. "Donald Sultan." *The New York Times,* December 1, 1985, p. C32.

Friedman, Ceil. *Donald Sultan Prints 1979–1985* (exhibition catalogue). Boston: Barbara Krakow Gallery, 1985.

Jones, Alan, et al. " 'Correspondences': New York Art Now" (exhibition catalogue). Tokyo: Laforet/Museum Harajuku, 1985.

Tomkins, Calvin. *Donald Sultan* (exhibition catalogue). Rome: Gian Enzo Sperone Gallery, 1985.

Henry, Gerrit. "Donald Sultan: His Prints." *The Print Collector's Newsletter,* January–February 1986, pp. 193–6.

Mango, Lorenzo. "Donald Sultan." *Flash Art* (Italian Edition), January–February 1986.

McKenzie, Barbara. "Art Review: Sultan's Work Has Substance, Vision." *Atlanta Journal/Constitution,* February 4, 1986.

Zaya. "La técnica de alquitrán-sobre-planchas-de-vinilo viaja al s. XIX." *Hartisimo,* March/April/May 1986.

Holm, Stellan. "Donald Sultan en amerikansk konstnär och hans hen." *Clic* (Sweden), April 1986, pp. 182–7.

"Sheep to Chevrons—April Offerings." *Art & Antiques,* April 1986, p. 35.

Larson, Kay. "Donald Sultan." *New York,* April 28, 1986, p. 97.

Carmean, Jr., E. A. "Summer Reading" (statement by the artist). *The Fort Worth Art Museum Calendar,* July–August 1986, p. 13.

Vedienne, Elizabeth. "Donald Sultan: La volupté du noir." *Décoration Internationale,* September 1986, pp. 135–9.

Hansen, Bernard. "Extremes of Art at Wesleyan University." *The Hartford Courant,* September 7, 1986, p. G6.

Lipson, Karin. "Art: Drawings That Magnify Mood and Mystery." *New York Newsday,* September 28, 1986, part II, p. 13.

Edelman, Robert G. "Donald Sultan at Blum Helman." *Art in America,* October 1986, pp. 158–60.

Raynor, Vivien. "Art: Brooklyn Show, 'Monumental Drawing.' " *The New York Times,* October 3, 1986, sec. 3, p. 24.

L.S. "Donald Sultan: Gentleman-Painter." *Le Matin,* October 29, 1986.

Ph.D. "Les nectarines de Donald Sultan." *Le Monde,* October 29, 1986.

Becker, Robert. "Confessions of a Young Artist: I Remember Pop—Donald Sultan." *Elle,* November 1986, p. 38.

"Monumental Drawings." *The Justinian* (a periodical for the Brooklyn Law School community), November 1986.

Chaillet, C. "Donald Sultan." *Elle,* November 4, 1986, p. 70.

Pradel, Jean-Louis. "Les citrons noirs de Donald Sultan." *L'événement du jeudi* (Paris), November 6–12, 1986, p. 106.

Dagen, Philippe. "Donald Sultan: Galerie Montenay-Delsol." *Art Press,* December 1986, p. 74.

Bianchi·Dessi·Gallo·Schnabel·Sultan (exhibition catalogue). Florence: Galeria Carini, 1986.

Master Drawings and Watercolors 1883–1986 (exhibition catalogue). New York: Barbara Mathes Gallery, 1986.

Maubert, Frank. *A propos de dessin* (exhibition catalogue). Paris: Galerie Adrien Maeght, 1986.

Rose, Barbara. *American Painting: The Twentieth Century.* New York: Rizzoli International Publications, Inc., 1986.

Turrel, Julia Brown, et al. *Individuals: A Selected History of Contemporary Art, 1945–1986.* The Museum of Contemporary Art, Los Angeles. New York: Abbeville Press, Inc., 1986.

Walker, Barry. *Public and Private: American Prints Today—The 24th National Print Exhibition* (exhibition catalogue). Brooklyn, New York: The Brooklyn Museum, 1986, p. 122.

Zimmer, William. "Works by Sultan and German Expressionists at Wesleyan." *The New York Times,* p. C28.

Zona, Louis A., et al. *50th National Midyear Exhibition* (exhibition catalogue). Youngstown, Ohio: The Butler Institute of American Art, 1986.

Muchnic, Suzanne. "Seeing 'Double' in Donald Sultan Exhibit." *Los Angeles Times,* January 12, 1987, p. 1.

Langley, Leonora. "Art Collector Profile: TV Producer Douglas S. Cramer's

Contemporary Art Collection." *Antiques & Fine Art,* February 1987, pp. 27–30.

Halpern, Nora. "Edye & Elie Broad." *Galeries Magazine* (International Edition), February–March 1987, pp. 87–97.

Gardner, Colin. "Santa Monica." *Los Angeles Times,* March 27, 1987.

Henry, Gerrit. "Dark Poetry." *Art News,* April 1987, pp. 104–11.

Russell, John. "Donald Sultan." *The New York Times,* April 24, 1987, p. C24.

Raynor, Vivien. "24 Artists and Friends in Kent Show." *The New York Times,* August 16, 1987.

Kogan, Rick. "The Little Girl and the Sultan." *The Chicago Tribune,* September 9, 1987.

Artner, Alan G. "Sultan's Tenet." *The Chicago Tribune,* September 20, 1987, p. 10.

Ligocki, Gordon. "Sultan's Work Should Endure." *The Times* (Hammond, Indiana), September 25, 1987.

Barnett, Catherine. "The Trouble with Modern Art." *Art & Antiques,* October 1987, p. 106.

Holg, Garrett. "Donald Sultan." *News-Sun,* October 1, 1987, p. 4.

Sherman, Mary. "Sultan's MCA Show Captures Urban Chaos." *Chicago Sun Times,* October 11, 1987, p. 4.

"Artsmart." *Harper's Bazaar,* November 1987, p. 122.

Russell, John. "Donald Sultan." *The New York Times,* November 20, 1987, p. C32.

Dubin, Zan. "Sultan Draws from the Past and the Present." *Los Angeles Times,* November 22, 1987, p. 100.

Knight, Christopher. "Sultan of Style's No Master of Art." *Los Angeles Herald Examiner,* November 29, 1987, p. E8.

Spector, Buzz. "Reviews: Donald Sultan." *Artforum,* December 1987, pp. 123–4.

Frank, Peter. "Haute New Imagist." *Los Angeles Weekly,* December 4, 1987.

Combes, Chantal. *The New Romantic Landscape* (exhibition catalogue). Stamford, Connecticut: The Whitney Museum of American Art, 1987.

Donald Sultan (exhibition catalogue). Interview by Carolyn Christov-Bahargiev. Nagoya, Japan: Akira Ikeda Gallery, 1987.

Dunlop, Ian, and Warren, Lynne. *Donald Sultan* (exhibition catalogue). Chicago: Museum of Contemporary Art, 1987.

The Monumental Image (exhibition catalogue). Rohnert Park, California: Sonoma State University, 1987.

"In Brief . . ." *Elle,* January 1988, p. 164.

Kazanjian, Dodie. "Lining Up for Art." *House & Garden,* March 1988, p. 33.

BARBARA ROSE

Barbara Rose was born in Washington, D.C. She attended Smith College and the Sorbonne, graduated from Barnard College, and received her Ph.D. from Columbia University. She has been the recipient of a Fulbright fellowship and many writing and film awards. Rose has taught at Sarah Lawrence College, Hunter College, Yale University and the University of California at Irvine. The author of *American Art Since 1900* and *American Painting: The Twentieth Century,* she has written and edited articles, monographs, museum catalogues and anthologies. A former contributing editor to *New York* magazine, *Art in America, Artforum* magazine and other art journals and curator for the Museum of Fine Arts in Houston, she is currently a consultant to *Partisan Review* and a member of the Visual Arts Committee of the Spanish Institute. Her most recent book is *Autocritique: Essays on Art and Anti-art.*

Other books in

ELIZABETH AVEDON EDITIONS

VINTAGE CONTEMPORARY ARTISTS SERIES

LOUISE BOURGEOIS

interviewed by Donald Kuspit

FRANCESCO CLEMENTE

interviewed by Rainer Crone
and Georgia Marsh

ERIC FISCHL

interviewed by Donald Kuspit

ROBERT RAUSCHENBERG

interviewed by Barbara Rose

DAVID SALLE

interviewed by Peter Schjeldahl